The Camel Theory
Design and execute your unique value proposition

Marco Lucchina

Copyright © 2017 Marco Lucchina

All rights reserved.

ISBN: 978-19-81096-04-6

Publisher: Independently published

CONTENTS

Introduction	1
The proposition	7
The proposition's ecosystem	21
The change	33
Leadership	45
Strategy	49
The Camel Theory	55
Business is for human beings	59
The benefit	71
Qualification	75
What	83
Why	97
Why-us	111
When	119
The Camel Way	125
Conclusions	133
Bibliography	137

Marco Lucchina

INTRODUCTION

Dear Reader,

I would like to thank you for your trust and, most of all, for giving the **'proposition'** your attention and the importance it deserves.

Allow me to start with a brief introduction that will be helpful for understanding the meaning of this book. To do so, I will borrow an example from the movie, "The Wolf of Wall Street", where Leonardo Di Caprio challenges a friend to sell him a pen. The moral of that scene is that if we were to sign a multi-million euro contract, we would be willing to pay a hundred euros for a pen. It's a matter of **perceived value**; that is, the quantification that we arbitrarily assign to an object, based on its usefulness to us. This particularly favorable situation can be either a coincidence or the result of a strategy. A successful proposition works on the latter to make "something" look irresistible.

I see this book as a "manual for myself". It is the result of years of revised notes and ideas, which I would like to share. I developed my knowledge in the more practical domain of *Information Technology,* but it is equally applicable to other contexts/markets.

This book is structured into two parts: the first containing general principles and ideas for an organization that aims to create a successful proposition. Here, I will explain the steps to get there and tell you which books you can read to give your study more depth.

The second part is about the Camel Theory, which is the combination of an organization's competitiveness, effectiveness and efficiency, seen from the proposition's point of view. In this part, we will see how the *Value Proposition* becomes **The Camel Theory** and how **qualification** is the key to success. What makes this innovative is the inclusion of choice mechanisms, which come from our human/emotional side, into the process of qualifying an opportunity. You can find additional documentation and all the maps on my website: www.thecameltheory.com and you can even satisfy your curiosity about where the name came from …

I strongly believe in language's ability to give concepts a context; each term has a precise meaning. This is why I often start with the semantic value of a concept and then broaden it, following the synecdoche's (the part represents the whole) rhetorical path, until I find a definition. This definition then becomes the starting point of the logic that connects theory and practice. Moreover, I believe that the traditional structure of management books, where each chapter is divided into a few pages, full of theories and analysis of examples, is not what we need here. Since I have no limitations in how I construct this text, my goal is to provide theoretical ideas, which are supported by simple examples and not by long studies. This will allow everyone to apply them to their own reality.

I hope I won't come off as too academic. However, I'll take the risk, and will write this book as if it were a graduate thesis, focusing the introduction on the current economical/cultural context, which also happens to be the "author's initial point of view".

Innovation and technology are two words that are often found together, because of the belief that they are synonyms. Technology or, more correctly, having the most advanced technology, is a crucial competitive tool for achieving your goals ahead of the competitors. A semantic analysis helps to clarify the concept: "technology" means "the cataloging and systematic study of techniques, often meaning a specific field or sector." A "technique" is a set of rules used to "do" a certain thing and it involves the adoption of a method and a strategy, which will help one to identify one's goals and the best means to achieve them. These goals are, in fact, the technology. Therefore, technique and technology are closely related; so much so that they are often confused with each other.

The first Industrial Revolution marks the split between "invention", which has always been present in human history, and **"innovation"**, which, from that moment on, changed mankind's way of life, so much so that it could be called a "revolution". The term "invention" refers to the discovery of a specific technique, whereas "innovation" designates its application. The invention itself does not cause change, but its widespread and constant application does. There is some similarity between the meanings of "innovation" and "technology" and, consequently, the ability to "master" a technique becomes a competitive factor. Progress and industrialization have introduced a third element: the product, an object which has benefits for those who use it; however, these benefits can only be enjoyed if their application matches them. If we want to reap all the benefits of an innovation, we must adapt to its terms of use, first. This means **changing** the way we do things. However, if we try to avoid change, and attempt to use the product's innovative aspects within the same context as existed before its invention, it is very unlikely that we will obtain the same results.

Industrial revolutions greatly accelerated technical and scientific progress, but every science develops from its past. Thus, the particular stage (of development) that one generation achieves becomes the starting point for the next.

The protagonists are engineers, businessmen, and dreamers, who are men of their own time, who are influenced by the social and intellectual structure in which they grew up and worked. Furthermore, innovators are not all the same in terms of skills, talents and inspiration. Each of them must learn about the developmental level, where their phase of science was situated, at the time they set out on their path. Some of them merely learn and disseminate; but, there are others with exceptional drive who can control innovation's direction, answering positively to the challenges they inherit from their predecessors. When combined, people, and the environment where they work, are factors that can either favor stability or **encourage change**.

In the 1990s, information technologies (IT) led to developments that were probably bigger than those, which we previously called "industrial revolutions". Today, IT has become so pervasive that it is to be found in every industrial process and in almost all of our daily activities. Its founding feature was speed; from that moment on, everything became faster and the evolution of technology, of which IT is an essential and inseparable component, is becoming even faster.

Now, in the second decade of the twenty-first century, we are witnessing constant change. Each new technological application creates new *businesses* and changes or destroys others. The adoption and dismissal curves have become very rapid, and a company's size is no longer enough to spare it from change. This is why we speak about ' *start-ups*', which are defined as new enterprises and which are supposed to be temporary in form. In fact, we can categorize their path in few steps: an idea is developed and, then, if the idea becomes widespread, the enterprise grows exponentially. If, however, the idea is good but is not autonomously sustainable, either the company will be purchased by a bigger one or it will fail. In all other cases, it is destined to close after a short time. We are living through a fourth industrial revolution: that of **digitalization,** which is changing many, if not all, of people's habits.

Out of the two concepts, transformation and digital, the key one is transformation, because it implies change. It also becomes innovation, if we take an active role in it, instead of just living through it. We see markets changing all the time, because of the introduction of an exceptional product or a model that changes the standards. The lowest common denominator in this is the use of technology to get it done.

Within the current market context, the words, "create value", "customer needs", "innovation", and "competitiveness" recur time and again. It is incredible how, in an interconnected world, these words are used with no elaboration. If we analyze the situation more carefully, we will see how both traditional companies and new ones, i.e., *start-ups*, need a market space, where they can specialize and become *leaders*. Once we are aware of these goals, we must redefine and recreate our "needs". After all, to be a *leader*, you should not follow anyone. You cannot conform to any predetermined plan. A *leader* is a leader because they have done something extraordinary, and that which is extraordinary, once complete, loses its extraordinary nature and becomes ordinary[1].

---

[1] Seth Godin, *Purple Cow*, Portfolio, 2003

THE PROPOSITION

The **proposition**'s goal is the creation and subsequent transfer of **value**. The meaning of value is a keystone; if we look in the dictionary[2], we'll find: "a fair or proper equivalent in money for something sold". Therefore, through the proposition, we create "something" (a set of benefits), which someone is willing to pay for.

Value is the equivalent, in money, of a customer's perceived value of a product's/service's functionality.

We will talk about a *proposition*, rather than a product or service, in order to maximize the idiosyncrasies of both: the perceived value of a service and the distribution of a product. In this way, when we approach a potential customer, we will be able to convey a higher value (that of the service), using simpler communication and a promotion that is aimed at the end-user. According to the

---

[2] https://www.collinsdictionary.com/dictionary/english/value

business model's perspective, this means having scalability of resources and revenue.

Companies that produce software are examples of this. Over the years, they have gone from being paid, simply for the time they spent writing code, to being paid for the functionality of the final product. Alternatively, there are the organizations in the training field that focus on results and the participants' experience. Likewise, if we need to refurbish something in our house, we prefer to hire someone who promises a result, rather than someone who will merely spend time working for us. Everyone believes that a results-based approach is more valuable.

A proposition is not just value. The extraordinary success of companies, such as Apple, shows us that a great **user experience** makes the difference between a good product *performance* and market dominance. The user experience serves to create a sense of **trust,** which the consumer needs to make the purchase, and to keep making it in the future, while firmly believing that they are making the right choice. In fact, this doesn't work by using rational components; rather, it constructs underlying layers of more simplified decision-making, which alleviates the stress we feel when we have to make a decision.

For example, when purchasing a *smartphone*, very few people are able to understand its technical specifications or to make a comparative table of its features. Most people will base their choice on other factors. We all associate Apple with a brand that produces amazing products that don't giveany problem; or, if a problem does occur, they have a customer service that isn't afraid to say, "Don't worry, Marco, we'll replace your iPhone with another one, straight away".

This "experience" makes us certain that it will always be like this with them: easy and satisfying. Unfortunately, there's only one Apple in the world, and although the stories we hear about them are truly phenomenal, we need to be aware that they're aimed more at dramatizing the possible than setting an example to follow. After all, we are talking about the inventors of the *smart phone* and the *App* ecosystem; those who gave us the chance to have an object in our pockets that is always connected and can process information and memorize data. They have triggered further revolutions, such as Uber, Airbnb and other spectacular *game changers*. However, the *user experience,* as we know it, was born in the Apple Store.

There are very few companies like them; only those with a global brand. Then, there are all the others: companies of different sizes that bring their message to the market through propositions. In this way, they aim to create experience, trust and success.

Some address the end-users as their customers, while others aim at professionals. We will concentrate on the latter; nevertheless, we will focus our attention on one point: the **human/emotional factor**. Business is done between people and, in their spare time, professionals are end-users; so, even messages that are destined for companies must be designed to reach people, all of whom have their own experiences and emotional baggage.

Nowadays, end-users take products' characteristics and functional advantages for granted, as well as the company's quality and positive image. What attracts them is the commercial proposition, good communication and a marketing campaign that dazzles them, touches their hearts and inspires their minds; something that offers an **experience**.

User experience has been *the* real *game changer* in the past few years. It is concerned with the realm of experience; i.e., a user attributes meaning and value to their possession of a product and their interaction with it. This also includes their personal perceptions of other features, such as usefulness, user-friendly-ness and the system's efficiency. It's the sum total of the emotions, perceptions and reactions that people feel when they connect with a product or service.

In other words, it equates to the degree of **subjective** conformity between one's expectations and one's satisfaction. So, in order to be effective, a proposition needs to be a combination of a service's value and a product's distribution. This is possible if we can reproduce the same effects, as the *user experience,* in companies. This is a feature of the proposition, it starts from successes with end-users, understands the causes and the mechanisms, and then re-applies them to B2B (an acronym for "Business to Business", that is, a company that wants to do business with another company). It's simply a matter of recreating that feeling of **trust**, by working on subjective perceptions, but using different communication channels. Trust will ensure that the promises made in the proposition, will be kept after the transaction has been concluded. After all, the *user experience* is really just a guarantee of future consumer satisfaction.

In the B2B world, trust is created, mainly through **relationships**. In fact, it's through relationships that a product/service achieves the same results as a *user experience*, the first of which is the guarantee that what you are about to purchase will satisfy your fundamental needs, or simply match the promises made before the sale; i.e., before the product/service is actually tested. A relationship of trust between people prompts a similar relationship between companies. B2B-oriented companies spend a lot on their sales' departments, while those whose business is primarily B2C ("Business to Customer") invest more in marketing and communication.

For example, a customer might only know a salesperson, who has just changed companies. The customer may trust that salesperson's word and, therefore tries a proposition from the new company where the sales person went to work. A previously kept promise, trust in the choices of a known person, familiarity - all of these are sufficient conditions to remain faithful, while the customer waits to see if their trust has been well placed.

This works because of the way people interpret it. The human factor is crucial to a proposition. This means that when we talk about the creation and transfer of value, we must not only think about the company that will acquire them. Above all, we need to think about, and propose, them as real benefits for the person, who is deciding to risk choosing us, in order to get value for their company.

Because of the way the human mind's decisional mechanisms work, an emotional component is always present and strong; personal benefits have a greater influence than business ones. The value map generated by our product/service needs to move in two directions: the most obvious one is towards the organization, and the more concrete one is towards our intermediary. The first direction must be present, otherwise trust and the relationship would lose their necessary **ethical** meaning. However, you can't even think about closing a deal simply by using personal advantages; that would put you at risk of a disciplinary or even a penal procedure. Once the ethical premise has been made, the value for the company can then be considered abstract, because what will be truly significant for the company will come from the perceptions of one or more people.

Now that we have introduced the power of the human component, we can state that:

*The **proposition** is a combination of the value generated by a typical service offer, but distributed in the form of a product, so that it may work effectively on the decisional mechanisms of our intermediary, who, being human, reasons and acts like an end-user.*

The transformations that software companies have undergone, as well as the revolution that Apple brought about with their "App Store", exemplify the development of the proposition: software's value lies in its ability to solve problems and digitalize processes. For years, companies thought about solutions first, and then looked for someone to create code. Then, software producers began to specialize. They hired skilled personnel who had expertise in areas, other than information technology, and they created packages to meet specific predefined needs. Consequently, they also needed to change their distribution channels, i.e., how a company reaches its customers. This was because the deciding factor was no longer just being good at writing software; the ability to solve specific problems was added.

Let's take an example: if a company decides to automate its warehouse, it will assess how "Software A" manages the process, assuming that the software is well written. At this point, "Company A" will not be able to attract customers by merely advertising its programmers' skills. Moreover, it will be interested in finding more customers, since it has already incurred the costs for creating the product, whereas before every new client meant hours of dedicated work. If we change the cost structure, the business model, the offered value and the distribution, the proposition changes. Now the company will need not just software, but specialized sellers, who are able to discuss the problems of warehouse automation with the customer. This is the distribution channel; the Channel Building Block of a business model that is described as a Business Model Generator[3].

In the Camel Theory's proposition, the channel will be a sales force that is oriented towards creating a relationship, as a key factor of, and a prerequisite to, the promise of value transfer.

---

[3] Alexander Osterwalder - Yves Pigneur, *Business Model Canvas*, 2010.

To complete our example; Apple's "App Store" or Google's "Google Play" are alternative channels that do not overlap and do not conflict with sales. Let's talk about why this is. "Company A" might decide to develop its channel and to create more software packages to sell through one of these *marketplaces*. In this case, it should also change its model and its target customers. These alternative channels are founded on their potential to sell relatively simple and cheap software to a large number of people; in this case, simplicity and price define the potential customers and the model. In order to be effective within this channel, the type of product must be cheap and should have a small number of clear functions. It's not a coincidence that the most downloaded paid *apps* are games, or *tools* that allow you to edit photos. What prevents "company A" from using the same model as the AppStore or GooglePlay is the size of the customer base, the value offered and, most of all, the possibility to **customize** the offer. Thus, we are talking about a proposition that's geared towards a specific segment; one which is able to accept the offered value. This is the space where the Camel Theory works.

The **Camel Theory's** proposition aims to build a method for addressing the assumptions we have looked at up until now: the creation of the value, the broadening of its perception and its distribution through relationships between people. This is a new type of **Value Proposition,** where the project and its execution belong to the same process.

What do we mean by a *value proposition?* A great reference book, to learn more about this, is 'Value Proposition Design'[4] by Alexander Osterweider. Besides recommending you read it, I would like to highlight two key passages.

The first one is the book's summary: a solution to the complex search for value propositions that customers want. It's a message that's intended for those who are overwhelmed by the task of creating value, who are involved in spectacular projects that were never realized or who are disappointed by the failure of a good idea. In fact, it's easy to misunderstand the concept of value. It is something that must be studied, understood and introduced into a methodology.

The second passage confirms the importance of seeing the customer as "a human being" inside a client organization; of understanding how human relationships are the foundation of business and, consequently, of realizing that a success proposition, is a transition point where a lot of energy has been spent.

When we speak about a proposition, the most difficult part is understanding the customer and, for this reason, it's recommended that you proceed one step at time. A proposition may have many starting points. It may be: an improvement of something that already exists,; a variation of something that's being offered to a wider customer base, a revolutionary idea for a new market segment, or a

---

[4]Osterwalder Pigneur Bernarda Smith, *Value Proposition Design*, 2014

technology for which we have exclusivity. Whatever it is, in order for it to become a success, it must be understood, and chosen, by its perspective customers. We do this by "listening to the customers" or, better still, "the non-customers". Obviously, this doesn't mean that we should just ask them what they want. It's a proven fact that they don't know what they want, or at least, they don't know how to describe it in terms that are useful for the person who is creating the proposition. Henry Ford said that if he had asked his customers what they wanted, their answer would have been "faster carriages"; nobody would have suggested inventing the automobile.

When we speak with people, details, which we might otherwise have underestimated, can come to light. People are precious sources of information. So many times, it is just a matter of having the right insight to start with. Many big successes started that way.

This is true of the Italian company Geox, a leader in the production of shoes. The company's founder based his entrepreneurial idea on the creation of rubber soles, which were waterproof but which would still let air pass through.

A few years ago, we faced the challenge of launching a new company, whose business was the resale of used computers. The idea was born from the success of some existing operators on eBay, together with a good availability of used computers, which were being "disposed of" with no thought for profit. Naturally, we started on eBay, which was a mistake. We tried first as private users and then as a store for used second hand goods, but it was all in vain. We didn't receive any orders.

There is plenty of information available online about companies and markets, with analyses and suggested business models, as well as information about the hardships some companies have encountered and resolved, or about success stories. The massive use of social network has transformed this information into a multi-directional stream, thanks to direct feedback from users. After a few hours of surfing the net, we become experts in almost every topic. Ridiculously, we may even imagine that we could have invented a Facebook or a Zara. Then when we read the biography of one of the richest men in the world, Amarcio Ortega, the founder of the Zara brand, we discover that he wasn't an expert at all, when he started out. So, what level of knowledge and experience is required to achieve success? Insight, knowledge and experience all make it possible for you to outline a framework for your initial ideas, but then it is necessary to face the market.

When starting work on a proposition, Alexander Osterweider[5] signposts three polar stars that you should always follow, so as not to get off track: **simplicity, consistency and prototyping.** Simplicity: since we are talking about a promise, this must be easily understandable and measurable. Consistency: our actions must plausibly match the image that we portray. Prototyping: even if we only have something partial, be it a function or the idea of a proposition, we need to find a way to experience it. This

---

[5] Alexander Osterwalder - Yves Pigneur, *Business Model Generation*, 2010.

is the key point. Never stop looking for feedback and make sure that it comes from every department in the company. Don't just stop at consultants or management. Managers are trained to make decisions early on and quickly, so they are not always used to the process of analysis or the development of ideas. They are decision-makers, the rational component of a company, as opposed to creatives. Your goal must simply be to develop ideas.

Make mistakes soon, so you can be successful sooner.

Testing a proposition is an art, and it should be done in the most rapid and inexpensive way possible, even before you have completed your model. Sometimes, simply exploring the customers' interest is not a winning move. It's necessary to discover what they don't say, what they desire but are unable to express rationally.

It was like that for us. We based our work on some other success stories and, almost immediately, we saw that this was the wrong way. Then, we noticed that those who bought our products commented very positively, when they came to pick up their purchase, about the fact that we were a big company with many years of experience in the sale of personal computers and relevant services.

Insight: our promise of value will have to be a used computer that was refurbished, by a big company, for the particulars of private use, so there won't be any risk for those who buy from us. In other words, it simply implies a procedure plus the relevant "refurbishment" certificate for the device, the possibility to return the product at any time and an unlimited one or two-year warranty. Considering our volumes, these wouldn't have been unbearable costs, but the magic was that people started to buy, trusting in our promise (and the positive feedback) and we had very few returns. We made a simple proposition, that was consistent with the company's image, and we had a prototype that allowed us to experiment quickly. Today, our business is doing extremely well and the only problem we have is finding enough material to sell. Indeed, the market is bigger than we can address.

In closing this chapter about the proposition, let's confirm that "customer need" is an extremely overrated concept, even if the customer must always be the center of every calculation. In addition, we must be aware that these needs are rarely described, and that the best ideas come from listening and gathering information. People are our most important data resource, but in order to read this data, we must keep an open mind, ready to receive the seed of an idea, and be in an organization that allows this seed to bloom.

Marco Lucchina

THE PROPOSITION'S ECOSYSTEM

In order to create and implement a successful **proposition**, a company must have some cultural and organizational principles: leadership skills, a predisposition to change and a strategy.

We will present the organization, metaphorically, as an organism that must prove it can "survive". It has to be able to face change or, put better, be able to change continuously, in order to deal with the challenges that continue to crop up. In order to do that, and to make sure that any problem can be dealt with and resolved, a company must have strong leadership and a strategy. This is the proposition's **ecosystem**.

A proposition is an expression of the values of the company that makes it. Values are a sort of "constitution" for a company. They hold it together and make sure that all the elements/individuals act according to a set of fundamental rules.

The first value that a proposition must acknowledge is **ethics**. A company that is based on honesty doesn't do shady deals to acquire new customers. Here, we are not referring to those extreme cases, where legal action is pursued, but simply to something, such as an unfulfilled promise: e.g., saying that a product can do something, when that isn't true. In fact, it's quite the reverse; an organization that adopts ethics as one of its founding values is able to create a proposition that includes psycho-emotional stimuli, which may act on (a customer's) unconscious decisional mechanisms.

Robert Cialdini[6]'s work is a landmark study on the mechanisms that produce acquiescence, which is the acceptance of a situation or a proposition. These innate, human mechanisms are determined by the combination of evolution and education. Every day, we all have to defend ourselves from a constant bombardment of stimuli, which comes at us from the environment with ever-increasing complexity and variability. To deal with this we resort to stereotypes, that is, to concise rules that allow us to classify things based on just few elements, so that we may react quickly and securely. What is interesting is that these "little rules" are the same for everyone, so it's possible to insert "activators" into a proposition that can trigger a decision. To understand this better, let's look at an example that Cialdini used at the beginning of his book.

---

[6] Robert Cialdini, *Influence. The Psychology of Persuasion,* 1984

An acquaintance of his, the owner of a gift store, noticed something interesting. Her co-worker made a mistake while pricing some souvenirs. Instead of applying a fifty percent discount on some pieces of bright-blue tableware, she accidentally marked them as double the original price. Incredibly, they were the best sellers of the week and, even more interesting, when the stock started to run out customers offered even higher prices to make sure they got the last pieces. Cialdini concluded that this was due to a "decision-making shortcut" that happens in the human brain to save cognitive energy. Effectively, something triggered one of the "automatic pre-set schemes" of action, in these people, that in most cases are supposed to help, but in cases like this, can create confusion. What happened to Cialdini's friend was that the erroneously doubled prices triggered one of the most common stereotypes: "expensive=good", and the products "flew off the shelves".

We may think that this could only happen to some silly tourists; but let's not underestimate the power of automatic behavior! When my daughter was born, I had already had years of experience in the study of "decisional shortcuts"; but, anytime I had to buy something for her, the "expensive=good" stereotype would come up in all its power. I tried to fight it rationally, because I understood what was happening. However, I wanted the best for her and this had a strong emotional impact on my rational decision-making mechanism. It effectively prevented me from buying cheap products and I justified it by saying things, such as "it's OK, anyways" or "she will get some use out of it". The only way I was able to solve the inner conflict was by purchasing expensive products with the rational assurance that their quality justified the price.

If we apply Cialdini's work to a proposition, we can state that in order to maximize the perceived value, we must understand the decisional/emotional mechanisms of the individual/consumer, who acts, at least for a part of their day, as a professional. The guarantee that these powerful tools aren't used improperly lies in the ethics of an organization, and its ability to transmit these to all of its employees.

Shared values are a common methodology among successful companies that are identified in McKinsey's "7s Model"[7].They are categorized as the interconnected meeting point of three *hard-skills*: strategy, structure and systems, and three *soft-skill*s: style, staff and skills. Organizations are made up of sets of interacting human resources. The glue that holds the system together is superstructures, which in turn have their own various interconnections. This is why shared values must be visible, clear and "measureable". They represent the organization's philosophy; they lead and guide the behavior of all those who belong to it.

Who would buy something from a company whose values were to maximize their profits at the expense of others? Nobody. However, when a proposition or a brand is the expression of a company's values, then it becomes

---

[7] Philip Kotler, Kevin Keller, *Marketing Management*, 2007

an identity, a factor of choice. For example, in 1998, despite the fact that its products "sucked", Steve Jobs[8] understood that the Apple brand still stood for "people who march to a different drummer; people who want the computer in their hands to help them change the world and create something that can make a difference, instead of just being a tool to complete a task.". In 1998, Apple was a company in difficulty, but their values were part of the brand's value. People chose Apple because they wanted to feel the same; they shared that way of thinking. Being able to offer them new products, which were beautiful this time round, was one of the reasons behind its comeback.

In companies, those who think up a **proposition**, from research and development to the marketing departments, are not those who will take it to the market. That will be the sales force's task. However, everyone must remember that a proposition is a **promise** that a company makes to its market; so, **everyone**, without exception, must actively contribute. In order for the company to be successful, the customers must trust it, and to earn this trust, it is necessary to respect the promises that are made.

Everyone must participate in the realization of the promise contained in the proposition.

In my experience, I've seen companies where there is little awareness of how a lack of (or an incorrect) proposition culture can damage the image and results of

---

[8] Walter Isaacson, *Steve Jobs,* Simon & Schuster, 2011

the entire organization, even when it only hinges on one small factor.

A while ago, while I was on a trip, I stopped in a *fast food restaurant* to get a hamburger and, obviously, to use the restroom. On leaving the toilet, I was horrified to be confronted with a sign, actually just a handwritten piece of paper that said, "Staff are required to wash their hands after using the restrooms". This is an example of how keeping the promise that the company made to its customers wasn't among anyone's goals, from the point of sales manager, who hung up the sign, to the workers who didn't care about their health and that of their customers. Anyone who used that restroom would leave the place before eating and wouldn't come back.

Oscar Wilde said there is no second chance to make a good first impression.

It takes a lot of time and energy to build the value of a brand and very little to destroy it. Even the behavior of a few individuals/elements can be harmful. That's why the values must bond together every part of the organization, whose corporate culture must be extremely pervasive and able to identify, and possibly expel, those individuals who don't adopt it.

Companies are complex objects that encompass a constant interconnection of personal interests and social dynamics. In the late eighties (of the last century), Gareth

Morgan[9] revised the image of a company, identifying it as an element that could no longer be considered the sum of all its parts. Models that compared companies to machinery, derived from Taylorism, failed in the face of the complex scenarios of market changes.

Within a context of continuous change, the centralization of decisional power and the investment of large amounts of time and resources, into planning every task, creates a paradox whereby the initial concepts become obsolete, even before their application. To avoid that risk, especially when success comes from one individuals' talent, it's necessary to replace a "**holistic**" approach with a "**systemic**" one. The first approach is characterized by individualism, by the belief that the individual can determine the result, while the second one affirms the importance of **relationships**: the more the individual influences the simplification of the relationships that constitute the processes, the more competitive the organization is.

The strength of this type of organization is its exchange of energy with the outside environment. In addition, the economy of Western nations has shifted from production to knowledge; we look for talented people with top résumés, even for positions that don't require them and we expect that their suggestions will improve the company and drive it towards growth. If people are not satisfied, they'll try to get on with their career. In any case, they won't

---

[99] Gareth Morgan, *Images of Organization*, 1986.

hinder the company or one of its departments, and will settle for what they have. If everyone is hungry, the organization will be a lot more dynamic, with a constant flow of energy. This is something that is unthinkable in a compartmentalized model.

Furthermore, in complex organizations there cannot be one single cause and effect relationship: neither results nor failures can be attributed to a single initiative. Systems are a collection of interconnected forces. Results are determined by changes in the balances, and not by a single action. That's why we need a **strategy**: a direction, defined by the *top management*.

Strategy is the force that allows the whole system to adapt, each segment according to its power and skills, but all pursuing the same goal. These organizations are "open systems", characterized by their exchanges with the surrounding environment and which trigger a continuous cycle: input, internal transformation, output and feedback. Conversely, closed systems tend to decline and fall apart. The self-sufficiency that growth produces is a process, based mainly on feedback. When organizations are faced with breakdowns and disruptions, they must act to find a solution and to establish a new balance.

The inner mechanisms of a system are as varied as its comparative environment: the reference market. So, the more competitive the market, the more complex the mechanisms and the more quickly people must adjust. A system's ability to evolve depends on its ability to adopt complex methods of differentiation and integration – in other words, **to change**.

The more an organization is able to handle the challenges of the market, the more it will evolve. The more it follows a developmental path, the more ambitious it will be. Ambition is characterized by constant dissatisfaction; this is the hunger, the fire, the fuel that drives the company to pursue goals that are ever more challenging. However, although ambition is a feature of a company, in order to prevent it from leading to disruptive forms of competition, it must be controlled through the **leadership.** Any set of human resources, which interact together, will need guidance.

Up until now, we have described the system as being characterized by a **balance** between its parts. That balance is maintained by a strategy, which is made possible through *leadership,* but change is always present and is targeted towards the system's survival and re-balancing. People will cooperate because everyone depends on each other, at least to some extent, to achieve results. In this case, there will also be no misuses of power, as the goal of every activity will be to support the system.

Let's look at an example: according to the aforementioned assumptions, not all collected euros will have the same value. Those that input energy into the system are more precious, as in the case of the sales, which leads to the creation of the volumes that facilitate decreasing production or supply costs. In this case, a strategic direction might be to sacrifice margins, in order to promote cost recovery or continued production.

Let's take the case of "Company T.", which operated in the market context of wired cabinets for data centers: a market that was dominated by a few big multinational corporations. This company would not have been able to compete on prices, so they needed to stand out from the quality perspective. They decided to include modules for specific equipment (routers) into their base price, something their competitors only included as an expensive option, and to focus on customization, allowing their customers to choose their colors and to apply their own logo. They also developed an innovative feature, a cabinet that included a cooling system, which aimed to appeal to the realities of those customers who may not have had a data center, but who still wanted to install hardware that needed intrusion detectors and controlled temperatures. Their sales strategy was to look for customers with these particularities, thus avoiding competing on the price of standard cabinets. However, their salespeople in the field did not adopt this strategy and, instead, resold the competitors' cabinets because they were cheaper and, therefore, offered bigger price-margins. Obviously, this brought the company to a crisis-point.

This is a case where values did not lead the company, and one component within it decided to take a different path, becoming rich (initially) but compromising the organization's survival. On the side, the other part of the company wasn't able to change or to produce a competitive product. Nor did they understand the sales' feedback. One part prevailed over the other, upsetting the balance. One of the causes was the lack of leadership from management and those who were in charge of the proposition. The fact that a company resells their competitors' products is absurd, in itself, and it's the obvious cause of the failure. However, we also need to consider the damage created by the conflict between those who wanted to focus on the price and those who had invested in the quality of the product, as well as the company's positioning, which focused on a niche market. Actually, the cause of the failure was the conflict generated by unshared values; what happened next was just a consequence. The sales department behaved like a closed system, prospering on its own for a while, until the lack of production ruined them as well.

Marco Lucchina

THE CHANGE

Gareth Morgan concluded that a systemic organization was similar to a living organism; like them, it relies on flexibility to adapt and survive. This metaphor also perfectly echoes Darwin's thoughts on the evolution of the species.

Individuals in a population compete with one another for natural resources; in this struggle to survive, the environment makes a selection that we call natural selection. In natural selection, the weakest individuals are eliminated; i.e., those whose characteristics make them less able to survive in certain environmental conditions. Only the fittest survive and transmit their traits to their offspring. In short, Darwin's theory of evolution is based on a few main points: variability of hereditary traits, inheritance of innate characteristics, adaptation to the environment, and struggle for survival, natural selection and geographic isolation.[10].

---

[10] https://it.wikipedia.org/wiki/L%27origine_delle_specie

As far as our study is concerned, the environment is the market, and one of the most merciless environmental conditions is **technological progress**. Since the end of the twenty-first century's initial decade, digital technologies have created a *digital transformation* phenomenon, which has helped to accelerate change, so that, for the first time, it could truly be described as global. Nowadays, even geographical isolation, which could equate to a closed or regulated market, is no longer a guarantee of survival.

The image of an organization as an organism leads us to draw an interesting conclusion: "no organizational model is better than another, but there are some that are more appropriate, because of the challenges to be faced and the environment where this must be done".[11] The challenge is to find new customers, sign contracts, and sell products; the environment is the market context and the means to do this is the **proposition**. The inclination to change is inherent in both the organization and the proposition.

A systemic organization welcomes change.

It does so, because that change is a type of innovation (and evolution) of the perceived organism. It succeeds thanks to the organizational flexibility of a well-balanced system, i.e., not one that is compartmentalized. This type of organization changes quickly in order to adapt. After all, in a constantly changing environment, the **speed** with which decisions are made is a competitive factor.

---

[11] Gareth Morgan, *Images of Organization*, 1986.

The Camel Theory

Heraclitus said, "Nothing is permanent except change."

We are constantly changing the way we do business. We create new *business models* and at the same time abandon others, which have become obsolete. For every Netflix that appears on the scene, a Blockbuster leaves it. A business model represents the way a company makes money. A proposition is the means through which that happens; it is the promise of a transfer of value, which a company makes to the customer, in exchange for money. They have an inseparable relationship; they depend on one another; so, if one of them changes, the other must change as well. It doesn't matter if the change is driven by the model, in which case, the company will choose to change; or if it's the proposition, which puts a new market scenario in place.

Change is a cultural factor. We human beings are born with "low-level programming", which means almost all of us will deal with stressful situations in the same way. Given that, eventually, all will have to face a crisis; an organization, just like an organism, will act in the same way as human beings do when under pressure: it will do what it has always done, and seek refuge in its comfort zone. That is, unless it is trained to act differently.

Let's take martial arts as an example. Some movements are contrary to our instinct, such as turning our heads to the other side when we see a punch coming. If we turn our heads, then we won't see the blow coming anymore, so we won't be able to avoid it. We must train our bodies to act differently, to bend the knees, while we focus on the threat and raise our guard. In order for this to happen, when we need it to, we must practice these movements until they become automatic.

When the crisis occurs, an organization that is used to change will face it, by changing.

Companies that are able to live with "constant change" will be more appreciated by their customers, because of their ability to innovate, and by their potential partners, because of their dynamism and the career opportunities they can offer. Change creates a virtuous circle that attracts both new customers and talented employees. It improves the ecosystem and produces energy.

In his book, 'The Innovator's Dilemma', Clayton Christensen[12] predicted the idea of *digital transformation* almost a decade in advance. He analyzed some scenarios from the American computer industry of the eighties and nineties, comparing *sustaining technologies*, meaning the natural (organic) development of a proposition, and *disruptive technologies*. At first, the latter were low-performance, low-profit products, which had the potential to create new markets. However, what happened in the early 2000s made his book a reference work on the subject. Apple's introduction of the iPhone was a turning point, because through disruptive technology, a computer firm was able not only to enter a new market (that of mobile phones), but also to dethrone those who had been the undisputed leaders up until that point: Nokia and Motorola. Neither company exists today; information

---

[12] Clayton M. Christensen, *The Innovator's Dilemma*, HarperCollins, New York, 2001

companies, such as Microsoft and Lenovo, bought them out. Apple transformed the phone market into a branch of the personal computer market, eventually calling even this latter market into question.

The theory behind the 'innovator's dilemma' says that the most successful companies in any given technological context, are not able to perceive the threat posed by disruptive technologies', at a structural level and, if they do, then the rigidity of their decisional processes prevents their management from changing the organization's strategy in time. For them, it is inconceivable that they would revolutionize the product/service that generates most of their profits just because of a potential threat. Because of this decision-making criticality, Christensen stresses, "the success of any company in a technological context is, at the same time and with rare exceptions, the guarantee of its failure in a more technologically evolve done".

To develop this theory, the author used a logic that is developed on four principles:

- Big companies depend on customers and investors for their resources. That means that it's the customers and the investors, and not the managers, who determine how to spend the money.

- Small markets do not solve the growth needs of big companies. Large companies need to grow, and the bigger they are, the more important the growth in terms of absolute value. For this reason, their strategy is often to consider markets that are big enough to be attractive.

The downside is that they don't consider those markets that are generated by *disruptive technologies*.

- Markets that don't exist cannot be analyzed. This seems blindingly obvious, but it this that makes it impossible for the managers of big companies to see the implications of the introduction of *disruptive technology*.

- An organization's capabilities define its disabilities.

For example, Christensen was able to identify the internet as a technological infrastructure that could destroy many industries. Today, we can read about it in the history books, as well as the incredible acceleration that it was given in 2008, with the launch of Apple's App Store platform. It's hard to say who, besides its creators, really understood the importance of Steve Jobs' announcement, at the Apple World Developer Conference in 2008, which, in essence, defined the concept of the *smart phone,* as we know it today. Only later, did it become obvious that the introduction of applications, or rather *apps*, into mobile devices began a new era.

The iPhone didn't just change the phone industry, forever; it also changed our way of communicating, travelling, eating and shopping. Apps, whether distributed by Apple or Google, have revolutionized almost every industry; they are today's *digital transformation* platform. There's an app for everything, as a popular commercial said. As concerns Nokia and Motorola, nobody questioned the quality of their products; but their managers simply delayed their transition towards the apps' ecosystem (something that other Asian producers did - Samsung did it first in the Android world.) Once they lost their leadership, the fierce competition made it impossible for them to attempt any remedial strategy.

To be successful, changing is not enough. It is necessary to change and maintain the leadership.

"The Innovator's Dilemma" also laid out the foundations of the *start-up* ecosystem, almost two decades before it happened. Very dynamic companies, which focus on technological innovation as a competitive factor, are actually able to offer significant growth and to create new markets. The big companies, which understood the danger of *disruptive technologies,* realized that the solution was not to fight or ignore them. Instead, they saw them as an opportunity to explore new markets, and to update their own technological context. They supported their development and when they believed these technologies were mature, they were ready to integrate them. Sometimes they even created a department for them, even if it was simply to prevent their competitors from using that technology. These technologies became extensions of their own research and development departments.

In 2016, it was announced, on the cbinsights.com site, that Hewlett Packard Enterprises(HPE) had acquired SimpliVity. This was a start-up, which had been included in the "Global Unicorn Club"[13] and whose proposition was both an opportunity for, and a threat to, HPE. It used innovative software functionality, to reproduce the traditional servers, storage and networking architectures in

---

[13] https://en.wikipedia.org/wiki/Unicorn_(finance)

a cheaper and more scalable and flexible manner. Its hardware component was actually HPE's bestselling product, but the added innovation put the rest of their offer at risk. A customer, who implements SimpliVity, buys Hewlett Packard Enterprise's bestselling server in bigger quantities, but gives up the remaining part of the offer, where the higher margins are: storage and networking, whose functions are virtualized and delivered by the software. By buying the company, HPE gained the primary place in the hyper-converged infrastructure market, a segment that had been created by companies who had invested in innovation: i.e., in *software-defined computing, software-defined networks and software-defined storage*. These were all technologies that were potentially disruptive for the traditional storage producers. However, instead of developing their own answer, HPE chose to follow this technology's evolution and to acquire one of the leaders in the field, as soon as they saw its success.

For large corporations, start-ups are a form of prototyping of the proposition.

In this way, big companies are able to handle a possible disruption of their market. But, what about the smaller firms, who can't make such investments? Their numbers and possibilities for investment change, but they must achieve the same results. Their main goal is also to increase innovation: so they need to invest their resources into improving products/services that are already successful, instead of wasting them on new projects that, statistically, are more likely to fail.

One problem is that when a new product becomes successful, it may undermine the current one. However, everyone can tackle this problem through **prototyping**: even if they cannot buy companies, they can always create groups of people, who are disconnected from those in charge of the main products, and who can explore new opportunities and test new propositions. Steve Jobs said that "innovation is not a matter of research and development's budget", but a way of thinking, of facing a problem by freeing the mind from the patterns that created it in the first place.

In 2006, Amazon was investing huge amounts of its resources in developing the web platform that supported its online bookstore. One feature of e-commerce portals is sizing, based on the peak loads, because performance must be guaranteed, at all times. Amazon had to size its information systems as if it was always handling the same number of orders that it received in December. Back then, it wasn't possible to purchase external load capacity, only for when it was required. However, those dealing with that problem had an interesting idea. If we can't buy the extra capacity that we need, in the months with more sales, we can sell the surplus of those months when we don't need it. That is how Amazon Web Services was born. The team in charge of this new business model was completely separate from the rest of the company. A few years later, Amazon Web Services would become the technology that made it possible to create a new market, *the public cloud,* a concept that threatened the sacred cows of the IT industry. Born as a prototype, *the public cloud* became the fastest growing sector, in only ten years' time.

We see markets changing, all the time, because of the introduction of an exceptional product or a model, capable of changing the standards. No market is safe from the possible introduction of a new technology that could turn it upside down. There are also many opportunities to invest in testing new propositions. So many resources are just one click away that trying something new is cheaper than doing nothing. Even though it is becoming more difficult to spot future forecasts/new trends, this doesn't make them any less inevitable.

A 'change attitude' allows us to adapt to new scenarios more quickly. We can't change what we do without changing the way we work. A disruptive innovation will never originate from a product/service's normal evolution and the success' factors that worked in the past are obstacles to the future. Change is a cultural factor, related to a moral impact that should not be underestimated. Martin Sykes[14] suggested three main reasons for people to accept change: to improve an existing situation, to achieve something new and useful, or to satisfy a desire or a personal motive. A person who drives change is motivated by incredible enthusiasm; they believe they can have a determining influence on things and this prompts them to invest more and more energy into it. Conversely, those who undergo a change will try to prevent it at all costs.

---

[14] Martin Sykes, N.Malik, M. West, *Storytelling & Visual Design*, 2013

They waste energy fighting the change, causing frustration and bad business results.

Therefore, prototyping is an effective strategy to manage change of the proposition.

> *Change is the first form of innovation.*
>
> *To continue innovating, leadership is necessary.*
>
> *The proposition is the means through which leadership is brought to the market.*

Marco Lucchina

LEADERSHIP

A leader is such because he did something extraordinary, and that which is extraordinary, once done, becomes ordinary[15]. A leader must keep his position at the top; unfortunately, if he is surpassed, he can't be considered as such anymore.

Leadership is what keeps a systemic organization together. It guides the individual choices of employees, who are the hubs of the system and it depends on the quality of the people that exercise it. It is not a form of control. Actually, according to Kenneth Blanchard[16], a leader's effectiveness doesn't determine what happens when he is present, but rather, what happens when he is absent. Semantics, particularly Latin, helps us to understand the essence of *leadership*.

---

[15] Seth Godin, *Purple Cow*, Portfolio, 2003

[16] Kenneth Blanchard, *The Leadership Pill: The Missing Ingredient in Motivating People Today*, Free Press, 2003

Under Roman law, the word, *auctoritas,* meant "authority" in terms of a person's influence, and was a characteristic with which the highest officials of the State were endowed. In the *Tabula Hebana, auctoritas* is a quality that derives from the charismatic power of divine inspiration. Therefore, it is suitable for supporting and directing the task of rational research. Even when it is not supported by the strength of political institutions, it still confers "authority "on any idea it puts forward. In fact:

Influential are those, who have earned such influence as to be followed.

Prestige is earned in the field. It's achieved through (at least) three factors: honesty (ethics), team spirit and the acknowledgement of others. It's not necessary to be authoritarian to be followed, but rather, to be authoritative and to be able to build a vision and **inspire** people.

The *leadership team* must use their influence both internally, so that people can work better, and on the market, through the proposition. One cannot exist without the other. The promise that a company makes to its customers will be influential and **winning,** only if the organization has pervasive and determined values.

Those values allow success to be quantified. **Profit** is the reward that comes from treating the customer well and creating a motivating environment for personnel; in the long run, it guarantees sustainability, product innovation and the assurance that there will be sufficient resources to solve problems, even in case of serious mistakes. A proposition that isn't meant to be profitable is doomed to fail. It's not a coincidence that, in every market, there are two or three companies that are successful, while others just plod along. This is related to the "Blue Ocean[17]" strategy, according to which, if we can't be among the leaders, we should change direction: we need to innovate and open new market segments. **Honesty** is the basis on which trust and respect are founded. An honest leader exhibits those same qualities that they would like to see in others. Similarly, others tend to accord trust and respect to those who behave in a way that reflects the values they have declared. The proposition benefits by contributing to brand value.

Trust comes from a match between values and behaviors. The key to leadership is the relationship that is constructed within the team. In order to be one, a team must share joys and pain. Reaching the summit is easier when you climb together. The proposition does the same for customers; the benefits it offers must be tools for the individual and professional success of those who choose it.

To do that, a leader looks for **excellence** for their company, and refuses to settle for anything less. A manager's task is to refuse anything that is not satisfactory, and to motivate their collaborators constantly to seek solutions. Overcoming the objections of those who tend to settle is a matter of culture: a winning culture. That is what determines the value of a company and the customer's perception of the (amount of) attention they

---

[17] W. Chan Kim - Renée Maunorgne, *Blue Ocean Strategy*, Harvard Business Review Press, 2005

receive. In a systemic organization, where the people who demand the best from their co-workers have key roles, even the customer will benefit. The company's culture will ensure that nobody, at any level, ignores a customer's dissatisfaction.

Leadership cannot be delegated. All the operational tasks, the tactical choices – those that are necessary to win the daily challenges – can be left in the hands of co-workers. However, a leader will never delegate their essence: that is, indicating the direction in which to move, motivating the team and, above all, the option to decide not to follow strategic guidelines. In my previous example of the sales representatives who preferred to resell their competitors' product, we saw the reprehensible results of a lack of leadership.

Within the ecosystem, a few hubs (employees) show the direction. Everybody else does everything within their power to obtain results, and they do that because they are united by shared values that allow them to be a team, an organism. The *leadership team* is the group of leaders that a company has; it is not unusual to see groups composed of just one person. The *leadership team* defines the strategy.

STRATEGY

Von Clausewitz said that strategy is "the art of winning wars," while tactics are "the art of winning battles." Translated into the context of organizational management, we can say that the *leader* determines the mission, which metaphorically is the war's goal, while the frontline management determines the actions to realize it.

Strategy and tactics are essential for the success of any firm. They are the theory and practice, the elaboration and execution, the mind and the muscles. Strategy must be the direction of an organization, *leadership* is the guide and shared values are the glue that keeps it all together. Companies that rely on skilled employees will give them the power to think and interpret. If the chain of command is too long, this will prevent strategy from being applied. When there is no contact with the *leadership team*, the passion that drives the company is lost. A company's *leadership team* is in charge of delivering a strategy and balancing the system to enable excellence in execution.

Strategic thinking makes it possible to identify the cause of any event and to act accordingly. For example, if a company wants to reproduce a successful product, in its own context, it can't simply copy the products' functions. It will have to identify the main reason for the product's success first, and plan the necessary actions to repeat it. There shouldn't be any alternative to this. Like copying without understanding, unplanned actions or plans elaborated by different advisors, only have one chance of success: luck - and in business, it's better to rely on oneself, on one's own skills, rather than on luck. When faced with a complex, unclear situation, the best choice should be waiting, understanding, and then acting. This doesn't mean being undecided; in fact, quite the opposite. It means analyzing, looking for more information, understanding and, once again, **experimenting**.

Experimentation doesn't imply turning an organization upside down. Instead, it means doing those small actions that test the relationship between cause and effect. We want the result of our thinking to be the resolution of a problem - whether it arose from a crisis or from a desire to innovate - without risking compromising what works already. In medical science, we reach a diagnosis before we think about a remedy.

The Japanese strategy **Kaizen**[18], that of proceeding in small steps, is the reference literature for our strategic model of innovation:

Continuous improvement of the proposition and internal and external testing, as a way towards innovation.

---

[18] Masaaki Imai, *Gemba Kaizen*, McGraw-Hill Education, 1997.

It should be noted that this method became famous because of its management of production line quality; introducing procedures that have led to new performance and productivity standards. In our case, let's consider only the philosophical assumptions, and leave the practical application aside. Implementing a Kaizen strategy implies a strong motivational drive and a sense of belonging to the company, so that the interests of the individual match those of the group to which they belong. One abandons individualism for an organicist vision, which is typical of eastern societies (*a systemic organization held together by shared values*).

It is a developmental model that retains the simplicity and solidity of its origins –incidentally, the same elements that are the strengths of *startup's*– and extends them to its operational and management teams. PDCA (*Plan, Do, Check, Act*) is a circular model that leads to the standardization, like the transformation of a service into a product that we addressed in the proposition's concept. The metaphor of the organization as an organism reflects the Kaizen image well: in fact, both aim to balance the system, despite the fact that they have significant and often opposite drivers, such as those for innovation and efficiency recovery.

The other three pillars of Kaizen are: quality above all; the use of concrete data for analysis (after all, before starting with the *problem solving*, it is necessary to complete the p*roblem defining*); and awareness that, at the end of the process, **our real employer is the customer**. As an aside, let me underline that the organism-organization's profit-multipliers are the particularities of its individual elements (employees), personalities, desire to excel, and intuition. If they match the values, and are used to apply a strategy, they can compensate for organizational gaps as well as maximizing opportunities. Let's not forget people's talents, even while we are discussing the system's theories.

In the early 2000s, Nintendo faced a difficult challenge: how to be profitable in the videogame consoles' market, when it was dominated by Microsoft and Sony, with their Xbox and PlayStation, respectively. Its product, the Nintendo GameCube, hadn't proved successful and the next version, the seventh generation console[19] would have to be a turning point for the company. The *leadership team* understood that relying on competitive factors, such as performance and advanced game play would have been useless; no matter the quality of the final product, there was no room in the Red Ocean[20] of the consoles' market for three actors with comparable products. Moreover, it was a specialized market, where expert players had histories with at least one of the two competitors; this alone seemed to make the challenge, of persuading players to change their gaming platform, impossible. The only way to survive in that world was to apply a "Blue Ocean Strategy." In December 2006, they launched the Nintendo Wii console, which, ten years later, had sold 101 million units compared

---

[19] https://en.wikipedia.org/wiki/Seventh_generation_of_video_game_consoles

[20] W. Chan Kim - Renée Maunorgne, *Blue Ocean Strategy*, Harvard Business Review Press, 2005

to the 85 million of their direct competitors, the market's apparently 'sacred monsters': Microsoft Xbox and Sony PlayStation. In the end, things went as planned; the almost-190-million-strong 'consoles for expert-users' market had been split almost equally between Microsoft and Sony, but the difference came from another ocean - a market of almost 90 million consoles, owned by non-expert players, who had never thought about video-game consoles as entertainment before. Nintendo's *leadership team* developed and applied a winning strategy. In 2004, they had already launched their portable console, the Nintendo DS, with relative success; but most importantly, they understood that they had attracted new customers with simplified game play. They decided to focus on this aspect for their new product, and invested everything in a new functionality: sensors that would allow the player to play while moving, thus activating a real, physical three-dimensional space. That functionality allowed gamers to play sports, such as tennis and bowling, by making the same movements as in the real game. This made the console usable by everyone, without them having to become experts with complicated *pads*. The *value proposition* was "a console for all," a promise that was emphasized by the initial price which included two games that were specifically designed to enhance the product's competitive advantage: the sensors that reproduced real movement, in space, within the videogame. The offered value, which was very well-received by the market, was that all the family could have fun, playing videogames. Personally, before the Wii, I had never been able to take my parents bowling. Finally, I was able to do that, and without leaving the house. In addition,

I can still remember, with pleasure, dinners with my friends, where the digestion was bolstered by Wii Sports. I was an expert player, and the Wii was my third console, so I can testify that it created a new market.

Applying strategy to the proposition, thinking in Blue Ocean terms: these are factors in which we can invest, so that the generated value creates or opens a new market. At the same time, the organization must be able to develop its *core business*; thus, triggering a process of continuous improvement.

A proposition's ecosystem is a strategic point of view; the summary of the various concepts of proposition, organization, change, leadership and strategy. A good organization ensures that what the strategy has outlined occurs. Its attitude to change is its first answer to crisis scenarios. The *leadership team* of a company is the person, or the group of people, who are in charge improving the organization and proposition, while the *management team* takes care of their maintenance. In this context, the thinking scheme that must be applied, in every situation, is that of a cycle, based on: understanding, design, realization, management. Testing can be added to each of them every time it is necessary to validate a change. The productization of the message implies specialization: we can excel only in a limited number of things and the global market contest rewards only excellence. We don't accept anything less than that.

The Camel Theory is established in an ecosystem like this one.

THE CAMEL THEORY

The goal of **The Camel Theory** is to develop a unique and winning **proposition.** We do this through a methodological path of *design* and *execution,* inside an ecosystem like the one we outlined, earlier in the book - where all resources act based on the same assumptions and with the same goals. By resources, we mean the people who design, execute and sell. The Camel Theory is a recommended extension of the *value proposition* concept.

The Value Proposition is a difficult thing to carry out. It represents the promise that a company makes to its reference market. Often we tend to confuse this with a company's individuality, working only on differentiating our competitive factors, where we have invested so much. However, these are not all the elements. It is a mistake to start with your product/service's qualities and to try to make them match the customer's "needs". Regrettably, these are rarely concrete or measurable. So, we end up operating in a context that is too general, and too unplanned. What are the main reasons for requests, that is, what are the decisional factors that lead customers in one direction over another? How can I apportion my energy so that I achieve the maximum result with the minimum effort? The Camel Theory answers these questions, and it does that using a scientific approach.

There's an anecdote that, without offending anyone, provides a nice caricature of an ineffective approach. There is saying from Lombardy (in Italy): "men and peacocks are the most stupid", referring to the fact that relentlessly imitating the peacock's love call, causes it to be in a state of constant sexual arousal. In this condition, the bird tends to fast to the point of wasting away. Jessica Yorzinski, a peacock researcher at the *Purdue University*, observed this bird in one of its most embarrassing moments: showing all its male attributes to the wrong species. The peacock showed its plumage, bent its head down and exploded in a series of obscenely loud squawks, as it headed towards the object of its desire (including the famous fanning out of feathers), only to discover that the object of its desire was a squirrel. Obviously, things did not go well. The squirrel quickly took off.

This rather bizarre example shows, metaphorically, the mistakes that an inexperienced seller makes, when they rely only on functionality. When they are faced with what they assume is interest from a customer, they don't hesitate to show all their competitive factors, those in which the company has invested a great deal, hoping that they will be enough. Without a method, however, only a small percentage of aspiring sellers will succeed and that will be because of their natural personal qualities, which attract the customers. Nature has graced them with characteristics that help them to face the situation, unconsciously: congeniality, availability, and adaptability. Unfortunately, a company can't rely on only a few employees for its success.

I did not use this example by coincidence. It is a nice, although possibly misunderstood topic that points to the power of stories. Besides, we know that all new ideas, big or small, will encounter some kind of opposition, especially if they require a change. In order to change a behavior, we must be clear, persuasive and accurate. **Storytelling**[21] is the tool that allows us to do that. Not only is the human mind able to elaborate just fragments of knowledge, but when sense and meaning are lacking, it can build its own vision, filling in the gaps with the information it possesses. The greater the complexity of the proposition, or if it requires specialized knowledge that the person we are speaking with doesn't have, the more likely it is that our interlocutor will create their own vision, which will be different from ours; thus rendering all the work we have done useless.

Storytelling allows you to use a story to build a "meaning structure," into which you can embed your proposition. A good example of this, and the way *storytelling* is used the most, is telling success stories. This technique makes it possible for people to choose us, through the thoughts, emotions and words of third parties. In order for it to work, the stories must be simple, real, and clear and they

---

[21]Martin Sykes, N.Malik, M. West, *Stories that Move Mountains: Storytelling & visual design*, Wiley, 2012

must be able to stir the right emotions to achieve the narrator's goal (for successful cases: united objectives).

Storytelling that is developed into a *storyboard* (a sort of catalogue of our stories) is a useful and elementary tool for creating visual stories. People tend to remember images better. Some studies show that 60% of an audience remembers information, which is included in stories, while only 7% remembers information contained in a list. To make this happen, the narration of an event, or a series of events, must have a form that can be visualized. It should be a clear and simple idea that can be visualized on a piece of paper, and whose goal is to guide a person, or a group of people, towards a specific conclusion.

To be effective, you have to impress people; you have to inspire them to act. In this way, you can combine motivation and energy. What is implied in a story makes it easier for people to act. We create a framework into which we insert our promise. This is what *storytelling* is about.

In the example of the peacock, we made fun of that poor animal, which chased a lure as if it was the love of its life, in order to make our listeners feel a mixture of grotesque and humiliating emotions that nobody would ever want to experience.

We will now embed the Camel Theory methodology into this framework. It is divided into four phases that represent the prerequisites and the sale, and which are packed with psychological principles to maximize its efficient acceptance.

BUSINESS IS FOR HUMAN BEINGS

Many choice mechanisms are unconscious, so it could happen that even when we show multiple features, randomly and without a strategy, a customer chooses us. This happens because we involuntarily trigger a **decision factor**. However, as much as experience shows that some people are instinctively led towards the right reasoning, this doesn't mean the sale was efficient.

We can't always put in our maximum effort into obtaining a result; it's exhausting. We need to make sure that the invested energies are the right ones, so as get the correct result. One of the most effective ways to do that is to work on the perceptions that influence the decisional process; Goleman and Cialdini's works show how a person's rational thought is subject to other emotional factors, both physiological and social.

In the introduction to his book, Daniel Goleman[22] proposes an interesting in-depth study of the morphology of the human brain, and offers a physiological explanation of the reasons why emotions prevail. All of us will have noticed that in those critical moments in life, the heart tends to prevail over the mind. This is thanks to the catalogue of emotions that was carved into our nervous system as our inner behavioral baggage, to ensure our survival.

Emotions are automatic habits, i.e., a pre-programmed action/reaction system. Within this context, it's important to note that all the new realities of our civilizations have arisen so quickly that **evolution**, which is a very slow process in itself, has not been able to adapt. The baggage of emotion and intuition, which we carry, drives immediate reactions, in a context where thought would be too slow. The structure of the human brain shows how the most ancient part (of it) is the emotional one.

Development starts in the brain stem, which surrounds the cephalic end of the spinal cord. The emotional centers originate from this structure, while the rational ones are supported by and depend on it. The first superstructure is the limbic system, and as it evolved, it perfected learning and memory. Then, a hundred million years ago, the neocortex developed, which contains those areas that interact with the senses and makes sense of what they

---

[22] Daniel Goleman, *Emotional Intelligence*, New York, NY; England: Bantam Books, Inc., 1995.

perceive; it's the place where thought and all human skills reside.

The neocortex gives light and shadow to our emotional life, even if it doesn't govern it, while the basic emotions are the prerogative of the limbic system. In human beings, the amygdala - a group of interconnected structures located above the brain stem - works as a storage place for emotional memory. For this reason, it is a repository of the actual meanings of events. It is also the gland that secretes the hormones that trigger the *fight or flight* reaction; it can detect the signals that come from our eyes, nose and ears before any other part of the brain. This allows the emotional system to act independently of the neocortex; information passes from the thalamus to the amygdala.

The hippocampus, which, among other things, transforms short-term memory into long-term memory, is involved in understanding patterns in perception. It remembers the bare facts, while the amygdala retains their emotional flavor. It could be said that our humanity is more evident in our emotions than in our logic. In a stressful situation, the emotional system acts first, so much so that the limbic system can take the neocortex "hostage," preventing the rational component of our brain from working. That is that unpleasant feeling you get when you feel very agitated and can't seem to reason.

In his book "Influence. The Psychology of Persuasion," Robert Cialdini[23] researched and identified six principles that lead to acquiescence. These principles

---

[23] Robert Cialdini, *Influence. The Psychology of Persuasion,* 1984;

trigger intellectual shortcuts that generate the automatic behaviors, which are necessary to live in an environment, which is extraordinarily complex in terms of stimuli. The principles are: reciprocity, consistency, social proof, authority, congeniality and scarcity. They act both physiologically and on an experimental level. Often, they use the emotional flavors, of the education and all the "instructions" we received during our childhood, when our rational element was developing, and for this reason we have a different, somehow increased perception of things. Just as, when we return to a place we used to visit as children, we find it smaller than we remembered it, an emotional event from our childhood will be memorized in our amygdala as more intense. Bringing it back to someone's mind, without the other person realizing it, makes it an extremely effective weapon.

Reciprocity. The principle says that we should reciprocate what someone else gives us. In fact, we are so compelled to return favors, gifts, invitations, etc., that in many languages, the term "obliged" has become a synonym for "thank you." According to Alvin Gouldner, all human societies share this norm. It is believed that a widespread and deeply shared sense of the future has made a huge difference in social human evolution; that's why it is as if the principle was written in evolution itself and possesses such a remarkable power.

The principle can be further reinforced by the "congeniality" effect, since that also influences the tendency to accept requests. People are more willing to do a favor for a 'nice' person, than an 'unfriendly-seeming' one. A good example of this is the practice of giving "free samples". Since they are gifts, they can call the reciprocity principle into question, in the same way as an unsolicited favor can trigger an obligation in the person who receives it. The effectiveness of the principle depends on the fact that, if we ignored the need to reciprocate, we would break the sequence and it we would be highly unlikely to receive other favors from this person in the future. To put aside possible future help, deliberately, goes against what evolution has handed down: this social context serves as a guarantee against future unexpected events. Consequently, we feel a sense of discomfort, amplified by the further confirmation of the group, which tends to attach labels, such as "opportunist" and "ungrateful." The principle is also triggered by "concessions": this occurs when, after an initial refusal, a concession is offered, such as a discount, or a product change. Also, in this case, the obligation to return the concession is what makes us concede something in return. In fact, this principle governs the process of forming compromises..

Consistency. This is, quite simply, our strong need to appear consistent with what we have done. Once we make a choice or a decision, we face many pressures, both personal and interpersonal, in our effort to be consistent with our commitment. This pressure generates responses that justify our previous decision. Once we make a decision, our need to be consistent drives us to align beliefs and impressions with what we have done. In fact, in our society, anyone who speaks, thinks and acts inconsistently is judged negatively, and is considered either a bungler or a liar. Consistency, on the other hand, is considered a sign of logic, rationality, stability and honesty. The key to triggering this principle is to make sure that the other person commits to something; their subsequent answers will be consistent with that commitment. The effect is amplified when we take a stand publicly, because power comes from the consideration of others towards those who lack this principle. Beware, however, that we must be convinced that the position taken was the result of free choice and without any pressure from outside.

Social proof. According to this principle, one of the ways we decide whether something is right is by finding out what others consider right. This principle is based on the belief that we make fewer mistakes if we act in line with what is socially evident. Moreover, the principle works best when that proof is supplied by the behavior of many people. The more uncertain the situation, the more we look to the behavior of others, believing it correct. The principle is reinforced by similarity; that is, when we observe the behavior of people similar to ourselves. In an almost empty parking lot, we prefer to leave our car next to another. We do that for no real reason other than we "think" that the other person had a valid reason to park in that place.

Congeniality. We tend to agree to requests from people we know and like. If these people are also good-looking, the positive advantages and the possibility of acquiescence rise. We tend to confer other positive qualities upon them automatically: talent, kindness, honesty and intelligence; and all this without even realizing that physical appearance is playing a role. Moreover, for this principle, we are also more attracted to people who are similar to us, and the similarity may be in opinions, personality traits, backgrounds, or lifestyles. To activate this principle, we begin by simply identifying our interests, origins and background. Knowing that someone likes or admires us can be a powerful way of gaining our sympathy and our acquiescence in return. This also makes sense because we like things that are familiar and that are obstacles to change.

Authority. The organization of human society requires obedience to authority. A stratified and widely shared system of authoritarian relationships guarantees many advantages for the group. It allows the development of complex structures of production, trade, defense and social control - all of which would otherwise be unconceivable. In fact, I don't know of any social group that benefits from anarchy. From birth, we are taught that obeying authority is right and disobeying it is wrong. An example is that of medicine; a doctor's authority has more influence because of the importance we give to health. Often, our actions are more influenced by the title than by the person who carries it; one symbol that proves our automatic response to authority is clothing, e.g. a doctor's coat.

Scarcity. According to the principle of scarcity, opportunities appear more interesting, to us, when their availability is limited. One example is the higher importance we give to a phone call, compared to a face-to-face conversation; the possibility of forever losing what we are hearing on the phone makes it more pressing. Another example is how manufacturing defects, for example with stamps, makes some versions unique. In fact, it seems that people are more motivated to act by the fear of losing something than the hope of gaining something of equal value. This principle, like the others, works because of our tendency towards shortcuts. Knowing that the things that are more difficult to possess are usually better than more accessible items, we often quickly assess an object's value based on its rarity.

This principle also has its foundations in childhood and adolescence. The tendency to rebel against restrictions to our freedom, which we developed during those periods, stays with us for our entire lives. In fact, we have a tendency to desire what is forbidden to us, considering it more valuable. These principles work because, in the contemporary world, there's an overexposure of information. In the face of this, even a human being's cognitive ability (the one that allowed us to become the dominant species on the planet) is no longer adequate. Even in the big city, our brain works very much like that of simpler organisms - simply responding to stimuli. We have seen the acceleration, triggered by technological progress, which the industrial revolution gave to change. Then we saw how the human brain can't cope when faced with too many stimuli. Because of this, the human brain began to use shortcuts, based on pieces of information that refer to experiences in the past. Our body adopted this trick to save cognitive energy. Basically, we make a decision without analyzing all of the available data, but only a single, representative element of it. This element is rooted in that part of our brain that governs emotions and that cannot be governed by the rational component, even after years of practice. It's like computer programming; it is senseless to use a computer's computational power to have it recalculate an equation that has already been calculated; we only need to create a link to that result. Similarly, in order to be economic and bloody effective in our action, we must be able to put the right stimuli in the proposition.

A problem arises when, for whatever reason, the signals that trigger the automatic responses are no longer reliable and lead in the wrong decision. For example, mother hens only take care of their chicks when they cheep and ignore them when they are silent. Animals have a fixed scheme of actions which works well in most cases. If the cheep was to be falsely imitated in another object, the mother hen would treat this object as if it was a baby chick.

Something similar inhuman beings is the manipulation of signals by professional persuaders (let's not forget the result of that research into the poor peacock). It is not making use of the principles, which regulate our automatic responses, that is fraudulent per se; it's the fact that it leads us to make the wrong decisions. For example, if we use the principle of authority to show that a product has been scientifically proven the best, and this is true; then, there is nothing wrong. Quite the contrary, this helps the consumer because it gives them more information and endorses their investments. However, when the product is not the best, or if the research is false, using the principle becomes dishonest.

To sum it up, if the information used in the promotion of a product/service is not false, then using Cialdini's principles is considered ethically correct, by the author himself. Company values are the first brick in the wall against the fraudulent use of the acquiescence techniques.

According to Jack Welch[24], the key virtues are **truth and trust**. The proposition is a communication channel to prospective customers, so it must be filled with truth and trust. For this to be possible, the company must:

Incessantly seek the truth and constantly build trust.

Cialdini's work also provides us with a scientific basis for the **relationship**'s mode of operation. In the relationship, three of his principles are at play: reciprocity, congeniality and social proof. It's no coincidence that these are the same principles that are at work on brand value. In fact, using these principles, we can reproduce the consumer choice mechanism. They differ only because they work on a broader scale; between companies, their mode of operation depends on the actions of the people who build the relationship.

The proposition's ecosystem is the same; only the channel changes. New York agency Interbrand has been listing the 100 most valuable brands worldwide, since 2000. They observed that the lowest common denominator for the top ten are: the customer's centrality, which allows us to understand and often anticipate their needs; the technological content, aimed at optimizing the products and services' usage experience by edging more and more in reality; the flexibility and adaptability to change, which allows one to reinvent oneself continuously, despite the (often obligatory)legacy built into each brand.

---

[24]Jack Welch, The Real-Life MBA. *Your No-BS Guide to Winning the Game, Building a Team, and Growing Your Career*, HarperBusiness, 2015

The first time I read something about this topic, I thought, "Get off! The time of advertising is over. These days, we are all 'switched-on' consumers; those tricks are for the weak!" I was wrong. However, to understand it, I had to experience it for myself many times. The first thing that comes to mind when you're studying Cialdini is to try to break the principles deliberately and see the results with your own eyes. I already gave you the example of purchasing things for my daughter. Here, I'll just invite you to try to follow your logic only and then gauge how much discomfort you feel. It's not as easy as you think. As much as we have evolved as consumers, the messages that prompt us to buy have also evolved, whereas the triggers haven't changed.

Marco Lucchina

THE BENEFIT

"People don't buy a product, they buy what they can do (with it)"[25].

When he spoke these words, Steve Jobs was holding up the idea of **benefit.** The word itself comes from the Latin *beneficium* and it doesn't only mean favor or service, but also privilege or satisfaction. *Beneficium* also had a legal value, both for the Romans and the Carolingians, as it was the foundation of the patron-vassal relationship. This was a relationship between equals, which was built on an exchange: the promise of a service (usually a military one) in return for the possible using of a good. The circle of "peers" linked to a "senior" was the "clientele."

One of the most ancient texts that tried to regulate this relationship is the *De Beneficiis,* written by Lucius Annaeus Seneca, in approximately 54 - 64 AD. It's interesting to

---

[25] Walter Isaacson, *Steve Jobs,* Simon & Schuster, 2011

note how the author points out the **moral duty** inherent in fulfilling the role of "benefit giver" and how, thanks to its reiteration, a mechanism of **virtuous reciprocity** can be started. This mechanism is the foundation of society's balance and, thanks to a patronage relationship ,this "dissemination of virtues" leads to the personal fulfillment of all the actors. The key, from Seneca to Jobs, is:

To activate a cycle of mutual personal satisfaction, based on virtues that exclude malice.

Let's put this historical-philosophical discussion of the finer points away and try to repeat Steve Job's sentence again; this time after productization lets us eliminate the distinction between products, services and solutions, preferring a more inclusive term such as "proposition" instead. The previous assumption becomes:

*The **proposition** expresses the functionality that fulfilling a **need** generates a **benefit**.*

The arrival point of this interpretation is:

*A proposition is irresistible if it is **indispensable**; so, the customer will be willing to make the purchase no matter the price.*

Unfortunately, only a few people, for example the inventors of the iPhone, can say that they are in this position. All the others must work on the **perception of value** and the creation of a context. They must then put all the elements that relate to the proposition into this context, in order to present a clear, captivating picture of what is being bought, and why.

The variables used are the functionalities: what I can do and what does my prospective customer think. The Camel Theory broadens the *value proposition* methodology so that it involves the differentiators and the required "weights", to maximize "perceived value." We have already seen how the concept of "productization" is a simplification, capable of working on the consumer-like mechanisms of our interlocutor; now we also know why they work. Let's focus on the fact that the inanimate being called "the customer" is a person first, and let's look for an effective way, in terms of effort/result, to set the sale in process. Thus, by virtue of the emotional component, we can state that:

People don't buy our products/services, but, attracted by an idea and captivated by a story, they buy the way they think they will feel when using them.

For example, we can obtain this result through the personalization. In fact, when we feel that a product/service has been made for us, our perception of its value increases. It triggers a feeling of exclusivity, which in turn, activates the principle of reciprocity, and increases the price that we are willing to pay.

Part of the value of digitalization lies in its potential to create business models that are based on personalization; something that was previously economically ineffective. Nowadays, we can gather a great deal of information about consumers' habits, and can interconnect them in real time, to create propositions that are tailor-made for every single person. Additionally, and thanks to *additive manufacturing*, the production process made possible by the 3D printing, they can be realized, even when the production involves only one piece.

In this way, **selling** acquires the meaning of:

Helping people to achieve the fulfillment they crave, with regard to both what they have bought and their personal goals.

An action's cost-effectiveness is achieved through qualification. Many decisional mechanisms are unconscious, so it may happen that when we show a customer many features (of a product), even randomly and without a strategy, they choose us. This happens when we involuntarily trigger a decisional factor, as in the case of the broken watch that indicates the right time, two times a day.

"Qualifying" means characterizing; it indicates a significant and substantial element. This element will be the decisive factor that leads a customer to buy our new product/service. Identifying this element quickly, and acting almost exclusively on it represents the cost-effectiveness of the action, which is what maximizes the result.

Through qualification, I try to obtain the maximum result with the minimum effort.

QUALIFICATION

Qualification is a process that narrows down the number of options and simplifies the decisional process, to the point where it makes us appear unique. The Camel Theory develops in four phases:

WHAT - WHY - WHY US - WHEN

What = What do we want to sell?

Why = Why do the customer need to buy it?

Why us = Why should they buy it from us?

When = When will they make that investment?

These four phases have a single goal:

To link the need/benefit relationship to the functionality of our proposition; to give this relationship the proper weight in our prospective customer's priorities so that it will be convenient, and seal the result with our (differentiating) individuality.

The correlation between need and benefit generate an investment, an expense. Its importance to the interlocutor is (almost) assured and its individuality points to the system that created it (us). The phases identify two distinct moments. The first concerns the game of strategy: the choice of the battlefield. The second, which is the sale, is about the victory of that battle.

To maximize their efficiency, the four phases must be included in our planning and then applied in the execution (sale) so that they activate a virtuous cycle that, thanks to feedback, makes it possible to sell what had been planned, taking into account sales results.

This is the reason why the Camel Theory is both *design* and *execution*. In designing our proposition, we realize the functionalities that we believe will stand out in the competitive scenario where they will be applied, because they will generate a benefit that satisfies the needs, highlighted in the customer-target profile.

The Camel Theory is designed to have a strong impact on the person first, and then on the professional. Before we begin working on a single opportunity, we should create a **customer profile**, which is a map of the goals of all the elements, which are involved in the decision-making process. The fact that the adoption of our product/service will bring the interlocutor advantages, such as personal fulfillment, career advancement, or a reduction in stress levels, is a precious element.

It is intimately connected to the concept of relationship: this allows us to discover them, and their discovery and realization nurture the relationship. We have seen how and why

The relationship in B2B replaces and nurtures the user experience.

The creation of maps, based on such effective factors, makes it possible to prepare the way for a **transfer of value** and the establishment of a system. This happens because once the promise's assumptions have been accepted (thanks to the relationship), the transfer of value will become simpler each time; creating, as Seneca called it, a "clientele".

Creating a customer profile is crucial, because what we are proposing is not going to end up in just an empty container. Instead, it will interact with everything our interlocutor knows, or thinks they know, about the subject; with their own beliefs, doubts, their usual ways of gathering information and with their experiences. Nobody can weigh the pros and cons of a proposition with complete impartiality, based only on logic and rationality. Human beings make up their own minds using, mainly, their opinion and experiences: if we know what those are, then we will have a significant advantage.

Therefore, we cannot ignore the ground on which our proposition falls, since this interaction depends on whether our message will be ignored, twisted, overturned or unheard. In other words, we must have a realistic model of our interlocutor (potential customer).

Making assumptions (proto-roles) can be helpful. In fact, they allow us to start the task of profiling from a semi-finished idea. We can assume that, depending on the person's role, there will be more or less effective arguments, and **common experiences**. For example[26], we can imagine that we are in front of a person who has one the following proto-roles: informant, influencer, decision-maker, or saboteur. Since the proto-role represents a projection of the customer-target profile, whoever designs the proposition will outline the characteristics, for each of them, which they believe are the most useful for the product/service's features.

The real profile, on the other hand, must be created taking into account the costumer's personal goals and their empathic predisposition towards our proposition, and us. The meeting point between the design's prerequisites and the information, gathered in the field, creates a PROFILE-MAP[27]: This map must be compiled independent of the end user; whether it is a technician who's assessing the functionalities, a project manager, a member of the company's management, or the buying expert in charge of negotiations.

A key point of the qualification is the creation of a mental or written map of the interlocutors, of their roles and their involvement in the decision-making process. For each step, we point out confirmations of the proto-roles and its relationship to us. We gather as much information as possible, even online, on the company and on the market in which they operate; as well as information on

---

[26] The characteristics of these proto-roles are available on www.thecameltheory.com.
[27] Example available on www.thecameltheory.com

their difficulties or successes. Their activity on the social networks could also provide good hints to help us identify what our interlocutors try to do in their work and their lives; what Alex Osterwalder[28] calls "jobs".

"Jobs" are a person's goals. They fall into three types: functional, when they are limited to the performance of a specific activity or finding a solution to a particular problem, for example, adapting to a rule; social, when they are more in tune with the person's emotional profile and are related to acquiring power or status; and personal, when they are related to a specific emotional status, such as feeling well or confident. Their «job» affects our interlocutor's actions in different ways and our relationship with the person allows us to discover their significance.

Alternatively, value can be obtaining an advantage, solving a problem or reducing a risk: it is the benefit for which the customer is willing to pay. Value exists only ethically, when it is contextualized in an ecosystem: the company for which the person works and its decision-making process.

Some of the negotiations that we still use as negative examples, after many years, were caused by the fact that we didn't define the customer profile correctly. More specifically, it was because the person who made the decisions about the proto-profile, had personal goals that were focused an emotionally stable and conservative choice.

---

[28]Osterwalder Pigneur Bernarda Smith, *Value Proposition Design*, 2014

For three months, negotiations with Company G focused on the very innovative functionalities of the solution we were proposing: an HP storage infrastructure, which would have allowed the customer to complete nighttime batches, which processed the data of the components to be assembled before production, in two hours instead of six. Production could have started two hours earlier, which would have significantly increased their capacity to accept orders. The company was going exceptionally well and incoming orders were higher than the productive capacity could meet. A specific case was created with an interlocutor, who proposed themselves as the decision-maker; but, in fact, they were just an influencer. Honestly, as the negotiations went on, we got the feeling of the thing; but, not being used to the decisional map, we tried to handle the situation in a traditional way: by focusing on the facts. We were sure that such a clear benefit, related to a need for increased production, was a winner. Big mistake! We lost the deal and only later discovered that the decision-maker had chosen our competitor's product simply because it was produced by IBM. At that time, the company was still an institution in the *information technology* field, to the point that it fully satisfied the decision-maker's main "job": by choosing IBM, he protected himself from any negative feedback. If it had been made he would have replied, "Hey, I chose the best. The others could have only made a worse job."

Moral: the emotional and personal component always wins, even over a clear and measurable benefit. This happens because a human being's rational component is a superstructure of the emotional one; if a decision reassures us emotionally, we will find valid reasons (at least for us) to support it, with a rational justification. This is the application of the principle of consistency.

Knowing how important the emotional component is, we should consider investing a lot of time with our interlocutor, getting to know them, asking questions and, most of all, listening and finding their root-causes. We should ask "Why" many times. Focus on active listening. Since the functional jobs will come up with the proposition, anyway, while we are building the relationship it's better to play more in the field of personal ones. The better we get to know the person, and the more information we obtain for the maps, the more chance we will have to connect with them and to create an accurate customer profile.

Nothing is absolute in human relationships, so we need to be sure that those things, which appear to be advantages or hardships to us, are actually also that for our interlocutor. If we also get a commitment with this verification, then we will have the principle of consistency[29] on our side. At that point, we can stop gathering information and we will have at least one map. The principle of social proof also works in the customer's map: identifying reference figures (for example, trade union representatives) helps to find similarities for the profile.

If the emotional component of profiles has a major role in the decision-making process, the latter has different implications to approving procedures. This process' map

---

[29] Robert Cialdini, *Influence. The Psychology of Persuasion*, 1984;

must include the profiles of all the people who take part in it, for various reasons. In order for the scheme to be complete, we need to assume, or discover, which benefits they would get if they worked with us, and what they would get if they worked with others. After identifying the decision-making process of the company that we have set our sights on, and after drawing a profile of all the interlocutors, we can start to outline our proposition, defining "what we want to sell".

WHAT

The proposition is an idea that could come from various areas. Examples might be exploiting a technological trend; discovering a functionality that cannot be copied; leveraging a new partnership; improving the costs structure to lower prices; adjusting our proposition to a less crowded market segment; or leveraging existing relationships to extend the current proposition, or to support a new one with the same target profile.

In order for the idea to become reality, someone else must welcome it and gives it value. By using this qualification, the Camel Theory aims to make the proposition so irresistible that it becomes indispensable. In operational terms, that means

Increasing the perception of value to create an idea of indispensability in the interlocutor will make the proposition irresistible.

First of all the idea, or the promise must be **simple** in order to generate value. The qualification process starts when we are able to answer the question, "What do we want to sell?" People are not able to valorize something abstract; they need concrete, quantifiable examples. As an example, let's take the adoption of an energy efficiency technology, whose promise is to save money.

A few years ago, the light bulb industry led the market, from the incandescent lamps to *led* ones. To do this, they focused on the savings that would be made over the entire lifetime of the product, despite its initially higher purchase price.

The simplicity of the saving's calculation meant it could be used as a sales tool. Everyone could make the calculation themselves and at the point of sales:

SAVING = [(W used before) − (W used after)] * [energy cost]*[hours of light bulb use]

It's not a coincidence that the hours of use, which is the lifetime of a light bulb, are certified and printed on each box. From this, the return on the investment:

ROI=operational result (SAVING) / net invested capital (LED LAMPS COST)

Supporting the assumptions made in the Benefit chapter, people are not buying a led light bulb, but rather the saving that they can obtain from its use. This is the true value.

The "value" is not always so clear. For example, if we wanted to propose this technology for a ceiling light with a modern-design and constructed from fine materials, we would have to work on other elements; on what is "perceived" – which, by definition, depends on personal and emotional factors.

Steve Jobs was among the first to identify **benefit** as a way to make perceived value concrete. With the first Apple Mac, he had to sell a product that was more expensive than those already on the market were. He had a more beautiful, better performing object that did more; but, most of all, it promised that everyone could use it, not just electronics enthusiasts and experts. The promise of benefit (usability) was the value for which the customer was willing to pay. Benefit was derived from the functionalities and it earned value as it satisfied the needs of those who bought it.

In order to generate a benefit, the functionalities of the product/service must create an advantage or solve our interlocutor's problem.

The idea on functionalities can come from internal sources, when we have a solution in search of a problem, or externally, from the market, when we have a problem in search of a solution. In any case, it will have to be **related to a need**: i.e. offer an advantage, solve a problem or reduce a risk. Advantages describe the results that customers want to achieve. Difficulties are obstacles relevant to their activities. The risk level represents the state of mind with which they are willing to live.

The first step towards qualification is to determine the scope of our sales action. The WHAT phase aims at creating a **correlation** between needs, benefits, and functionalities, allowing us to work on just combining the functionality's rational elements with everyone's personal desires, through Cialdini's[30] principles. He affirms that

> *It is needs that prompt people to act. If we know their needs, we can increase satisfaction and persuade them to buy.*

Never underestimate the meaning of need, which should be differentiated from a necessity. The latter refers to a more advanced level of qualification, when the decision-maker knows what they want, has already analyzed and quantified it, and is able to discuss it clearly. This distinction helps us understand whether the decision-making process happened with or without our contribution. If we are able to intervene before needs turn to necessity, we are in the semantic area where needs are still unexpressed, implicit, and related to an emotion. Those who have to qualify a proposition should try to operate in this area, as much as possible.

In this way, we can gain an undisputable competitive advantage: we take part in the decision-making process and we can try to direct the choices, starting from the needs, towards those necessities that mapped the peculiarities of our product/service. Anticipating and taking part in the decision, of what a customer needs, equates to choosing the battlefield: the more it is qualified, the better it will be for us instead of our competitors.

For example, thanks to qualification, we will no longer have to deal with the kid who wants to buy a car with his

---

[30]Robert Cialdini, *Influence. The Psychology of Persuasion,* Kindle edition

first paycheck, but with a man who finally has sufficient resources to get that *status-symbol* he has been desiring for so long. The proposition's scope will be defined by the characteristics of what he considers a *status symbol*, while all the others will be general, and not qualified. They will be irrelevant to the decision. Conversely, those (elements) that match the profile, from alloy wheels to electronic gadgets, increase the perceived value and, therefore, the amount the customer is willing to pay.

The **WHAT-MAP**[31] is a tool that makes it possible for you to visualize this phase and to understand what the winning elements are: i.e. what our customer really wants to buy. On the left-hand side, we need to show how our product/service's functionalities transform into benefits. We need to order them so that the advantages are in in the top half, followed by solutions to potential problems. For example, how reduced energy consumption (functionality) becomes a saving (benefit). In doing this, we must consider how, because of the principle of scarcity[32], the elements that reduce difficulties are more powerful than those that generate advantages. In fact, the fear of loss prompts human beings to act, more than the possibility of gaining an advantage, even if, from a rational point of view, the latter is bigger.

On the right-hand side, we need to identify needs. Here, also, there are two possible origins. Needs may arise from the market, where they are the consequences of the

---

[31] WHAT-MAP available on www.thecameltheory.com

[32] Robert Cialdini, *Influence. The Psychology of Persuasion,* 1984;

personal assumptions of what "universal" needs are, made by those who operate in that market segment. For example, a sales agent who has to travel long distances, will need a comfortable and reliable car. Alternatively, needs may depend on the professional-human-being. In this case, we know that identifying their needs is much more complex, but it is also an area with more opportunities. An area where we can start to create a Blue Ocean[33], where the influence of the market is less visible to our competitors.

In order to be more accurate when we compile needs, we must understand our interlocutor, and to do that, we need to create a profile. There are many ways to do that; for example, the one proposed by Daniel Goleman[34]. The goal of this type of map is to identify the needs, motivations and desires of a person, through an analysis of what they say, think and do. The trail of consistency between these pieces of information allows us to draw a profile of the person: This profile needs to be more accurate than the one we created through assumptions, in the design phase. This one will include the personal characteristics of the person.

It's not something that is easy to do and it requires a lot of practice, however, the reward is motivating and proportional to the effort. Goleman suggests we train our **emotional intelligence**, which is our ability to understand

---

[33]W. Chan Kim - Renée Maunorgne, *Blue Ocean Strategy*,
Harvard Business Review Press, 2005
[34]Daniel Goleman, *Emotional Intelligence*, New York, NY;

England: Bantam Books, Inc., 1995.

others, their motivations, their desires and their way of working (or rather, the reasons behind certain choices). Empathy, a necessary capacity to draw up any profile, comes from understanding ourselves. Human beings share many common behaviors; the more open we are to our emotions the more we will be able to understand those of others.

It is empathy that will guide us towards what to include in the profile. If we listen to our interlocutor, we will be able to grasp the emotional nuances that will give significance to fact. For example, if we were able to understand frustration, while they are telling us about the hold-up in the system that they're responsible for, we could note, among the needs, "reliability" and "sense of security".

Feelings are rarely put into words, so if my interlocutor tells us that they want reliability, then we are probably in a more advanced phase than we should be; we're in the phase of "necessities". To be reasonably sure not to make a mistake, it is recommended that we ask them to tell us some of their **experiences** concerning the subject of our proposition. In fact:

Experience is the melting pot where need is created.

This is the starting point of the emotional profile. The PROFILE-MAP[35] is a graphic example of how to realize it. Its prismatic form allows the visual relationships that

---

35 Available on www.thecameltheory.com

exist between a proto-role[36] and its needs to be seen, as well. The compilation of this map is continuous, and runs across-the-board of all the qualification phases, and it moves forward through our knowledge of the customer and the relationship. Let's start by pointing out the empathic hints that we observed while we were speaking with our interlocutor.

The WHAT-MAP is useful for both the design and the execution phases; this double significance makes it possible for both those who design and those who perform, to work on the same assumptions. In fact, the map must be drawn from left to right by the designers, and from right to left by those who take the proposition to the market. Comparisons between the two activates the virtuous cycle of constant improvement. Like all the processes, it must be addressed with the idea of learning - constantly monitoring the results, documenting the cause-effect relationships and mapping which actions causes which reactions - in order to increase efficiency and to compile a list of the successful cases.

Certainly, we will encounter unexpected cases, both positive and negative; we will learn from experience and will update our maps. The more examples we will have, the more we will be able to make case lists (*storyboards*) that can become points on our map.

---

[36] The proto-role represents the characteristics of the target customer that were assumed in the design phase of the proposition.

A few examples of "needs" could be to: generate savings, in terms of money and time; eliminate frustrations or inconveniences; reduce risks, either operational or legal; avoid negative social consequences, bad figures, or loss of power or status; produce results that surpass expectations, providing better quality; beat the competition, in terms of performance; favor the adoption of a technology. In this phase, our goal is to identify needs in the profile and match them with the benefits, derived from the functionalities that satisfy them. It could be automatic (as for the light bulbs) or we may need to force things a little, with an action that persuades our interlocutor to make that benefit a necessity.

The six rules that Cialdini[37] identified, as the keys to persuading a person to accept a proposition are reciprocity, scarcity, authority, consistency, congeniality and social proof. When we choose the "promise" that we want to transform into a benefit, we should identify the principle used, and note it on the map. The "decisional shortcuts" that we will identify will be the glue between needs and benefits. They work because they recall an experience, which is rooted in our memory, to the point where they trigger an action and we don't even feel the need to dig any deeper.

Need is based on experience, and thanks to that, we can create a link to benefit, which constitutes the WHAT-LIST in the map. For example, in the case of systems reliability, telling a story about how someone else, with a

---

[37]Robert Cialdini, *Influence. The Psychology of Persuasion*, 1984;

similar profile to that of our interlocutor, avoided frustration by choosing our product/service would create a link between functionality, benefit and need. We only work on specific contents, because they are more interesting for people than generalized ones. To create a convincing story, we must take concepts and advice and turn them into concrete examples that are interesting to our interlocutor.

The ***storyboard*** is a map of all the *stories* that we can *tell*, whether they are success stories or hypothetical situations where the relationship between need and benefit was realized. It's an essential tool for executing the WHAT phase and it has nothing to do with PowerPoint or any other program of slide shows. We have an initial relationship with a person, through which we must find out what advantage that person wants to obtain or what problem bothers them.

We could certainly make the process quicker by starting with a barrage of personal questions, but the efficacy of this would be close to zero. In such a situation, very few, if any, people would give useful answers. In fact, such a situation would probably trigger a *"fight or flight"* reaction. We all have our own '*no-go-areas*', whether physical or mental, where no one may enter without permission. Crossing that boundary creates discomfort, which doesn't help the relationship or a potential agreement.

For example, if a stranger sat next to us, in a non-crowded environment, with a lot of physical contact, we would feel uncomfortable and we would react either by moving away (*flight*) or eliminating the intruder (*fight*). We feel something similar when someone asks us too many personal questions. Luckily, everyone has a variable no-go-area which can be progressively reduced through a relationship, fading as the relationship becomes closer.

Acting through the telling of facts, feelings or mistakes happened to others, the "stories" are the tool that makes it possible for us to reduce the risk of a *fight-or-fly* reaction. The principle of like-ability makes us like familiar things. Moreover, starting from our childhood, we are all used to consider the pleasant stories and the happy-end: it's better to hear a story told from the point of view of someone who obtained a benefit and a personal advantage, like a career advance or a higher visibility in the company.

The creation of a WHAT-MAP starts from a promise, and the virtuous cycle of a long-term collaboration depends on our ability to respect it, creating at the same time a new fulfilling experience. A promise that is the expression of the ecosystem that created it, our organization, and reflects its importance and credibility.

Credibility and trust are the virtues of resiliency, of a company's ability to survive over time. Building them up takes a lot of time, but they can be destroyed in a minute. Therefore, **never lie**. When we are speaking with a customer, we will inevitably be faced with questions such as "So, this product will allow me to…" or "Do you promise that it will solve all my problems?" We must resist the temptation to say "Yes", just because it seems easier. If we always say "Yes", we'll probably get the first order, but not a second one. On the contrary, being able to debate the reasons behind certain choices has its advantages, the first being reliability.

The WHAT-MAP ends with the identification of a **match** between our product/service's benefit and the needs derived from the market or from our interlocutor. We can expect three (maximum five) matches for each promise, but only one will trigger an action. The WHAT-LIST is extremely important, as the following phases will work only on these matches. For this reason, it's very important to use the principle of consistency as proof of the work done, and as insurance against any subsequent changes of mind. For it to be as strong as possible, it's necessary that our interlocutor affirms that these really are their needs. If he they do that in front of their co-workers, then we can be reasonably sure that they will do whatever is necessary to stay consistent to these affirmations. It will be hard for a competitor to change the field where we may confront each other. We chose it with the customer and others will have to adapt to it.

The WHAT-LIST is the **qualified scope of the proposition.** Now we have to shift our energies to persuasion, and to do that, we must work on motives, i.e. on the **why**. Cialdini[38] says that if we ask someone to do us a favor, we will obtain it more easily if we provide some reason: people like to have a reason for what they do. He made a study, where he simply asked people, who were in line to make photocopies, if he could go in front of them. He received a positive answer in 95% of the cases, simply

---

[38] Robert Cialdini, *Influence. The Psychology of Persuasion*, 1984;

by adding a reason such as, "I am in a hurry" or "I only have five pages to copy, can I go first?"

Marco Lucchina

WHY

The WHAT phase is the perimeter, which allows us to focus our efforts onto a smaller area, into which we channel all our energies, to maximize efficacy. The WHY-PHASE determines value; that is, the importance of the elements in the WHAT-LIST, i.e. the need/benefit relationship that is the result of the functionality of the proposition.

The WHY-PHASE establishes which factors are convincing enough to make an investment.

The WHY-MAP[39] is a visual tool that helps us to determine the importance of the benefits, so that we understand which one will be the **convincing one** to pass to action. In order to reach the WHY-MAP we need to filter the WHAT-LIST through the PROFILE-MAP.

---

[39] WHY-MAP available on www.thecameltheory.com

Benefits are important to varying degrees, which depend on the interlocutor. They are more effective if they solve a frustration or reward an ambition, since it is a person who makes the decision and therefore, their personal motives/beliefs matter most. A comparison between the empathic information recorded in the previous phase, and those of the proto-profile should enable us to verify the level of similarity quickly.

For example, my wife doesn't take energy saving into consideration, when she chooses a lamp. She is interested in the quality of the light and how, based on that, a lamp changes the color of the furniture and the walls. To her, the promise of LED light bulbs is potentially harmful, as they could activate the shortcut of "saving equals bad quality".

Obviously, the needs of one single person are not enough; it's true that they drive people to act, but since we're in a professional environment, choices must also be justified with rational elements. The benefits must be tangible for the organization and potentially quantifiable. For this reason, the WHY-PHASE is sub-divided into two macro-points: finding the convincing element and rationalizing the motives, quantifying the benefit.

As we try to understand what the convincing element is, we need to remember that the human brain is divided in two hemispheres: the left one is responsible for logic; it is pragmatic and rational, and elaborates information one piece at a time. It is the language center of the brain. On the other hand, the right hemisphere is instinctive and emotional; it mainly recognizes visual information and is influenced by spiritual and mystical aspects. Both hemispheres act on choices simultaneously, but theright hemisphere is undoubtedly used more; especially when there isn't enough information or when primitive elements, or elements associated with our childhood prevail, such as those activated by Cialdini's principles. Moreover, the left hemisphere prefers stability and prompts us to handle new problems based on experience, while the right hemisphere is where innovation and overall vision reside. Some scientists believe that, based on our job, we develop one hemisphere more than the other; which is why proto-roles are so important.

That's how we conceived the PROFILE-MAP: the advantages are on the right-hand side, because they can be related to that hemisphere, while the difficulty reducers are on the left-hand side. We positioned the proto-profile following the same logic. We grouped advisors, influencers, decision-makers and buyers on the map depending on the predominant hemisphere. The first two are on the right, because we assumed that because of their "proponent" roles, they would be relieved from their responsibilities and would be able to focus more on opportunities. Moreover, a change can bring many advantages to these profiles, especially if they have promoted it. On the other hand, buyers and decision-makers concentrate more on operational details such as obtaining a better price (sometimes even to the detriment of functionality), or the need to maintain functional environments and well-balanced relationships. They are more rational.

Recent studies[40] discovered that the relationship between the two hemispheres plays a crucial role in children with a high creative potential. When they solve mathematical problems, these "highly-gifted" children don't have the classic hemispheric asymmetry. In fact, when problem solving, they activate both hemispheres, whereas "normal" children have an asymmetry that favors the left hemisphere. In other words, the hemispheres of gifted children dialogue more efficiently and are both involved; they generate a high number of ideas or hypotheses from any given stimulus (the quality of fluidity is fundamental for creativity, because it allows reasoning to flow through the characteristics of one hemisphere or the other, depending on convenience) and easily alternate proposed solutions (quality of flexibility).

These skills are also related to a higher aptitude for research and the selection of which information is stored in the long-term memory, as well as a capacity for association and combing ideas. For this reason, we combined two proto-profiles in the PROFILE-MAP, which can operate easily between advantages and difficulties; they are the companies' top figures, and are very business-oriented. We will give more importance to quantitative elements, where they are concerned.

---

[40]Maud Besançon, *Le Haut Potentiel* Crèatif available on https://www.cairn.info/revue-enfance2-2010-1-page-77.htm

We will also add a curiosity: visual maps that are used to stimulate the right hemisphere and, therefore, creativity. Print out all the maps that you find on www.thecameltheory.com on A3 or bigger sheets and use *Post-it notes* to enter information. This will allow you to move them easily: you won't always put the right information on your first attempt. Often it will have to be moved between the various maps or set aside. The final result will be an additional stimulus to creativity and a simple understanding of the big picture.

Ideas will come up that are relevant to the topic at hand, as well as other topics. It's what David Sibbet calls "Idea Mapping". It's a flexible approach that starts with a blank sheet and helps to visualize the way of thinking and the planning. In fact, we begin with the imagination, which must be put on paper in order to become a shareable thought and we prompt others to evolve it; the evolution will lead to action.

At this point, we have compared the elements in the WHAT-LIST with our interlocutor's profile and their proto-role. We need to be able to detect the presence of the same element in all of the analyses in order to consider it the convincing element.

The interlocutor is the key, but often they are not the only one. It is necessary to create a PROFILE-MAP for all the people we were able to talk to, no matter if we had time to dig deeper or not. We recommend using the prismatic scheme[41] and filling it in during the interview or right

---

[41] Example available on www.thecameltheory.com

afterwards. Indicate what type of interlocutor this person could be and trying to figure out what advantages are among their goals or what problems they have to face. It can be a simple note in a notebook that we could improve if we had the chance to add more detailed information, or we could keep it as it is, giving it little importance.

All the PROFILE-MAPS must be included in the POWER-MAP[42]. The goal of this additional map is to trace a path, which is drawn from the information, in hand, about all the interlocutors involved in the decision-making process. To do that, we draw a profile of the people that we will have to persuade and we design a prism of goals, for each one of them, indicating their name and proto-role. We will note any missing profiles, as such, still trying to hypothesize how they will intervene in the decision-making process.

At this point, we have a semi-finished WHY-MAP. In the previous phase, we listened to our interlocutor in order to understand his needs as a person-professional. We compared those needs with the benefits of our product/service and we reported any matches in the WHAT-LIST. Thanks to the PROFILE-MAP, we were able to organize them in such a way that they fit the goals of our interlocutor's role. Now we must work on the **quantitative elements**.

A quantitative element what allows you to give value to the benefit.

---

[42]Example available on www.thecameltheory.com

In the light bulb example, the benefit's quantification is quite simple: how much time and money are saved. Using the same example, we should work with the interlocutor to understand how much saving is convincing for them. For example, they might be an environmentalist type, oriented towards the big picture of contributing to the good of the planet. In this case, even the smallest economy would be convincing. In that case, we would find more elements on the right-hand side of the prism. Conversely, it would take a significant saving to make a technologically-skeptical type change their habits and they would have more elements on the left-hand side of the prism.

What we need to do is give value to the benefit and to establish, with the profiles' help, if it is **convincing**. Sometimes, quantifying is impossible, or we can't establish if it is convincing. In these cases, we will have to go back to work on the perception. In this case, we can find help in another of Cialdini's principles, the principle of contrast[43], which acts on the **quantification** in such a way that, when we are presented with two stimuli, in successions that differ sufficiently, we tend to see the second one as more different than it really is.

This is the principle that governs the management of our product/service options. For instance, if our proposition was a laptop, complete with options, the first thing we should present is the computer. Once we have persuaded the customer to buy an object worth over a

---

[43]Robert Cialdini, *Influence. The Psychology of Persuasion*, 1984;

thousand euros, all the options, such as assistance contracts, external screens, etc., which usually cost a little over a hundred euros, will not seem as expensive and the customer will be more willing to buy them. It's more effective, for the seller, to present the most expensive item first; doing the opposite would turn the same principle against him, and make the item appear even more expensive. The principle of contrast recommends presenting items starting with the top of the range ones.

Returning to our work on the map, we have to organize the list, starting with the maximum potential benefit. In so doing, we present the return on investment in terms of benefit quantification and/or we do that in the most effective way for discernment. Now, in order to determine whether it is "convincing" enough to trigger an action, we use the principle of consistency[44]. We need our interlocutor to confirm the importance of these benefits **for them and their organization**. It's important for us to have a tool, to measure the work done; so don't be afraid to ask polite questions, i.e. those that are unlikely to provoke a *fight or flight* reaction, but that are precise and focused enough to **obtain a commitment**.

This commitment must be measured and monitored. Even the principle of consistency will fail, if assumptions change. For example, the managerial constraint that created the requirement may have collapsed, or our interlocutor may have obtained that position he longed for, thanks to another project. We are in the phase that

---

[44]Robert Cialdini, *Influence. The Psychology of Persuasion,* 1984;

prompts action; it can only be completed if our customer is persuaded that they must act, and that they must do so within a defined time limit.

To prevent the passage of time changing or disqualifying the work done, we introduce the concept of a sense of urgency. We will talk about this more in the WHEN-PHASE; now, what matters is to identify whether there is anything that might induce it: an event that prompts action.

There are many ways to induce this in the consumer: limited promotions, a date by which they can benefit from a purchase, or a product's limited availability, all induce a feeling of having to act immediately if we want to obtain something. This is Cialdini's principle of scarcity, where an object seems more desirable if it has a sense of exclusivity that comes from its lack of availability. On an emotional level, it recalls the world of collecting, which all of us have been attracted to at one time or another.

The effect of promotions is reduced in professional relationships. However, some **external factors** may intervene, which trigger a sense of urgency, such as a management directive, the threat of losing business, the obligation to adapt to a government disposition, a deadline, a new opportunity or the obsolesce of one's current equipment. The order in which these examples are presented is not random, but follows the levels of a sense of urgency. An obligation that comes from an authority not only reinforces the emotional state, using Cialdini's principle of authority, but it also leaves no options: we must go in that direction.

As the obligation becomes weaker, other elements intervene to distract us from action. For example, having an action plan or having made a decision could lower the sense of urgency's level, thus postponing the action. On an emotional level, "having a plan" is very close to "solving the problem". This could be a problem for us, as we have to close the WHY-PHASE. We need to intervene, and if the scenario changes slightly, we need to adapt to it.

Once again, Cialdini's principle of consistency provides a guarantee in this respect: we make sure that our interlocutor commits to us. We have already used this principle, when we added the search for an element that could trigger a sense of urgency. Now it's time to make them commit and "make the investment". If that commitment is both with us and with their organization, then the aforementioned principle would be reinforced.

We must be careful to read the context correctly. Nothing is absolute. As we've just affirmed, a decision can be changed. It's more difficult for that to happen once we have a commitment, as it is something personal. The interlocutor has invested themselves and their credibility, in bringing their social being to the table. Keeping one's word is a way for a person to be in a group; it recalls trust, in the fact that they will be able to help the group in the times of need.

A decision is based on rational elements, while a commitment is based on emotional ones. We must act on both. In fact, *we identify the benefit, we quantify it and then we ask for a commitment.*

Any external event that triggers a sense of urgency to act is only an opportunity if we have factored it the problems and the risks for which our product/service can be a solution. Otherwise, it's better not to take advantage of it. The Camel Theory is based on the assumption that design and execution are a continuous cycle and rely on the same foundations; therefore, our *storyboard* must include the necessary elements to **respond to the urgency**.

It may happen that a customer calls their supplier, because they have had specific instructions from the *management*, or they have overlooked a deadline and realize that they can't find a solution on their own. In this case, it's obvious that the first who answers "Yes, I can do it", will get the deal: imposing something with a strict deadline is a very strong convincing element.

It would be a mistake to rush in and improvise our scope of action, just to adapt it to the demand. Either the demand is consistent with what we defined in the design, or it's better for us to give a negative answer. If we don't have this **convincing element** in our *storyboard*, we must be clear with the customer; we won't be able to provide the expected benefit and are aware, that in this situation, we don't represent value for him. However, this actually lays the foundations for higher credibility in the future. In fact:

Success occurs when planning meets opportunity.

At this point, we just have to verify whether we are doing the right thing. The ultimate test is to ask ourselves if the customer "**cannot do anything**". It's not an easy question; we should be able to distance ourselves, so that our judgment is not be influenced by the work we've done up until now. For this reason, it's a good idea to proceed by setting up a "role-playing game". After studying the profile, a co-worker plays the customer, trying to reason on the basis of the same assumptions.

Two potential traps make this test necessary. One is the **false positive**, where we think that an event is convincing, when actually it isn't. The other one is the **false negative**, when we think that our proposition is not convincing. Both of these arise from a mistake in the needs' significance or in the interlocutor's profile.

An opportunity may appear bigger or smaller than it really is, because we are governed by the same emotional principles that we have described above. For example, a seller who's not meeting their quota will be nervous and will tend to see opportunities as bigger than they really are. This situation is similar to that of a gambler who thinks they can recover all their losses with one last game. They are persuaded that their plan will work; thus, the feeling of having a loophole lowers their stress level and they see it as even more of an opportunity than it is.

The predominance of emotion means the gambler doesn't give any importance to the rational information of the theory of probability, which tells them that their chances of winning are the same as they had in all the games they already lost.

Once the appropriate tests are completed, we will have qualified our proposition properly, matched the functionalities to the benefits that map our interlocutor's needs. We will have established the significance of each need, in order to find the **elements** that are **convincing for the action**. In case we don't have a clear element that could clearly trigger a sense of urgency, we have promised our customer that they or their organization will gain value from the benefits offered. We have filled in all the maps: the what-map, profile-map, power-map and why-map. We have verified that there aren't any technical issues that could put into question, even partially, the transfer of value, which was quantified. We have included a monitoring cycle, to control whether the perception of the various interlocutors changes and we are ready to act in case of a change in the scenario.

At this point, we have completed the WHY-PHASE. We can be reasonably sure that there will be a transfer of value, even if we are not sure (yet) that it will be with us.

Marco Lucchina

WHY-US

The WHAT and WHY phases were qualification phases, whereas the following two: WHY US and WHEN, are about **sales**. We have seen how we have a natural tendency to start at this phase, listing the functionalities of a product/service and/or our company's uniqueness, thinking this will be an effective sales' technique. Unfortunately, uniqueness has a high cost; and is the result of large investments, and energies that shouldn't be wasted.

In this WHY US phase, we will show that uniqueness only exists if the investments made during the design phase map against the qualification's results. If not, we will only have a "peacock effect".

The goal is that the assumptions, from the end of the previous phase, will be mapped against our competitive benefits. The **differentiators** that determined the choices we made about functionalities must now become **unique points** that will allow us to close the deal, and to gain a customer or a market segment. This connection is the answer to the following question:

How *does my product/service deliver that benefit?*

As an example; when Apple designed the first iPod, they focused on the digital use of its musical content. If we follow our reasoning, would have they been able to propose it as a better designed "MP3 player"? Of course not. I used this example because, in 2001, Apple was not the company we know it as today. They were still trying to improve their fortunes, after the hardships of the nineties and this product was an incredible accelerator for the company. Back then, nobody could say, "They are only selling it because it's trendy", so their promise was fulfilled, without the power that the brand has today.

Since Apple's targets were private users, the product's launch needed a qualification, which meant a slogan that comprised all the phases of the Camel Theory. They chose "1000 songs in your pocket". With this message, their qualification exactly mapped the uniqueness of the product: it was the first player to use a five-gigabyte hard drive. WHAT: digital music, downloadable from the internet; WHY: having music with us always; WHY-US: because it's the only product that can store so much music and be connected to an online platform (iTunes).

Conversely, when an idea comes from the market, others have already established the first two phases; so, our task is to understand the mechanisms and cause-effect relationships. It is harder to be successful in this phase than in the previous ones; we must win in the WHY-US-PHASE.

When HP acquired Palm, to enter the tablets' market, the operating system, WebOS, did not fit into any map, despites its being supported by a decent level of hardware. The applications were the WHAT, while their number and the quality were the WHY. Apple had already launched their message: "there is an App for everything": meaning editing pictures, booking a hotel room, having texting systems, and checking our social network pages with an interface that was simpler than the traditional browsers. These were the benefits for the end-users. HP's WebOS platform did not have enough applications available to satisfy users, so the question, "How do I get the benefit" didn't have an answer. In an already crowded market, they were invisible.

Microsoft's case was different. When they launched their Surface tablet, they made sure to support its uniqueness in both the qualification and sales phases: supplying a tablet with the operating system of a PC but with a keyboard. The WHAT was "to have two devices in one", and the WHY was "being a user, who travels and may need a tablet's functionalities, but who mainly works with a notebook". This type of qualification opened up a new market segment. How did the Surface deliver its benefits? By having the form of a tablet and the internal components of a notebook, and with a keyboard incorporated into the cover. It was the big success, which all the other producers copied thereafter. The investment was engineering a PC that had the dimensions and the shape of a tablet; no small thing, but thanks to the alignment of the WHAT and the WHY it became a "blue ocean" moment.

These examples prompt further consideration: in order to succeed, the differentiators should be perceived as unique. In fact:

Uniqueness is the characteristic that makes us stand out from others as more able to deliver the expected benefit.

This is closely linked to the decisional factor; it broadens the perception that only we can respond to the need. Seth Godin[45] said that he didn't know what the key factors for success were, but he knew that the one way to fail was to try to please everybody. Therefore, we can only be unique in a few things and they must be chosen: specialization is a consequence of the qualification process. Even amazing characteristics, which are outside the area of our discussion, are, at best, irrelevant.

In the previous examples, we used consumer products to underline the importance of qualification as a prerequisite for sales. In the previous chapters, we saw that the difference between the consumer and the professional markets is mainly the channel. In the first case, qualification was made by the message, the promotional campaign, the brand value; whereas, **the relationship creates the seller in the professional market**. Everything else remains the same. There is a consumer

---

[45] Seth Godin, *Purple Cow*, Portfolio, 2003

behind every professional and their personal motives are stronger than their rational ones.

Examples of this are more difficult to find in the professional world, because they are more specialized. However, there is a stronger connection between price and value. There are several reasons for this. Firstly, because we are selling something more complex than a product, the price is often not public, but is built based on an estimate. Then, there are the different elements that may cause the price to change significantly. All of these possibilities pass through the interlocutors - the sellers, who must be able to reproduce the marketing results, on the end-user, through the relationship and the qualification.

The choice of the battlefield is crucial for any strategy. In the case of the proposition; knowing, in advance, that the functionality of our product/service is connected to its uniqueness, we have, in fact, led the customer to see our organization as having a unique value that can satisfy their needs. The **perceived value** is the customer's global evaluation of what they are getting in relation to what they are giving. It's such a powerful aspect of our work that it overshadows the price, because it includes it.

The perceived value can be defined with the formula:

Perceived Value = Communicated Value * Actual Value

We have seen how much the world has changed; we have many more options for choice, but less time to evaluate them. Unconsciously, we look for shortcuts to make the right decision, since we don't have the time, and often the tools, to do it.

If we work on the lever of communication, the perceived value becomes a decisional shortcut. The actual value can't change very much, not unless additional and significant investments are made. However, the communicated value leaves us with room to maneuver. We work on this to create exclusivity.

The communicated value depends on the skills of the person who argues on its behalf, as well as the passion and the *storytelling* associated with the proposition. It's a direct expression of the proposition's ecosystem and is transmitted by people, everyone must know it. In the ecosystem chapter we saw that successful companies must employee skilled people, who can interpret the story of **how** the organization is unique for **that** task with passion, dedication and style.

Storytelling empowers uniqueness

Good *storytelling* is able to create a sense of exclusivity. Having the chance to work with a successful company is an example of this. Successful people are liked; the same cannot be said for arrogant ones. Another element is customization. With good *storytelling* we will not only be "unique", but we will aim to be unique specifically "for that customer". After all, we are willing to pay more for a tailor-made suit than for something we just picked out a store, even if it's well-made.

The level of customization is not important; what matters is that the interlocutor *perceives* it as "made for them", according to the messages that they receive, as a consumer, where the experience has been created expressly for them to feel unique. It is impossible to predict the level of customization of our proposal; it could be almost all or nothing. In any case, the advice is to communicate it as a factor of great exclusivity.

We should include many elements about **how we deliver benefit,** in the *storyboard*; in this way, we strengthen the uniqueness and at the same time we explain how our organization works to achieve success for both parties: the customer's and ours. This element is a direct result of the actual value, but it is also a great catalyst for perceived value. We have already attracted our interlocutor with the benefits that they will receive. They will just have to be persuaded that they will obtain them more quickly and with guaranteed results, by using our company. If told the right way, showing something close to a unique experience, associated with an entire organization that works with passion, dedication, and professionalism to satisfy requirements, can transmit a sense of exclusivity that makes that proposition irresistible.

At this point, we can reasonably claim to "have an irresistible proposition".

Marco Lucchina

WHEN

Quality and time are tightly connected - how and when we deliver a benefit. They epitomize the sales process. Delivery times are the ability to keep the promise of the delivery of value.

Because of the intrinsic connection between when we design a proposition and when we execute it, the time that we deliver the benefit must also be predictable, so that we can answer questions effectively. These elements are defined in the design phase, because they are part of the idea; part of the value. For example, a product that is in stock and another that has still to be produced will have different delivery times, of course. The activation of a service may require a different time again. Our duty, under the promise we made, is to respect these times.

In order for this to work, it doesn't depend only on our company's efficiency, but also on the customer's expectations. Both of these must be aligned. This is the time to verify that there aren't incongruities and that we can reasonably use this information as a basis to establish the exact deadline. We must clarify the delivery time for each personalization required, any those customizations must not change the delivery times significantly.

This is the **negotiation** phase; where we agree on prices; that are the quantification of the value, the time and the criteria to evaluate the quality of the work when it is done. It's time to close the deal.

The WHEN-PHASE is not only preparatory to forecasting our company's results; it's the conclusion of the job in all its components. It's the moment when all the expectations are about to be realized. What would a "peacock" do in front of a customer who affirmed their interest in our product/service? It would wait. That would be a mistake. We have worked to make sure that all the pieces are in their position on the chessboard: now it's time to act, to close the deal. To do that, let's depend on a sense of urgency.

From a more emotional point of view, a **sense of urgency** is a state of mind that prompts someone to do something. Previously, we connected it to the benefits and its function was to prompt our interlocutor into making the commitment that those benefits had a value for him and that they were convincing. Now, we must use it to gain a commitment to a signature. Continuing to use *storytelling* about "how we deliver the benefit", will help us to instill the idea that in order to obtain that benefit, **the expected time must be respected**.

In the WHY-PHASE, we saw how to identify those events that might persuade a person to act. If their deadline matches the delivery time, we will be in the right place to close the WHEN-PHASE. This works well because it is combined with the principle of scarcity: we assign a deadline, beyond which we will not be able to guarantee the same benefit. For example, many sellers use the end of the quarter as a deadline for the validity of any extra discounts they have offered.

We have come a long way, and we have discovered, or helped to determine, what the customer will buy, why they have to buy, and why it is better that they buy from us; always with the accent on exclusivity and reliability. Both elements will guarantee a signature on the order and on schedule. We are now entering the most critical phase of the negotiation, one where we will be more emotionally liable to make concessions whose impact we will only realize later. In order to preserve the work we have already done, we must **be able to say no.**

It is extremely difficult to say "no" to a customer. On an emotional level, it causes anxiety about the result, because we worry that denying a concession, we will damage the work already done. However, in many cases, what happens, instead, is the opposite. Your "no" should not be arrogant or presumptuous, but which is always supported by reasons that are consistent with the company's values and the qualification process. We have worked professionally, sharing all our assumptions with our interlocutors and only moving to the next step after receiving the confirmation that what has been done is approved. Looking at it this way, a negative answer to requests that are almost impossible to realize, or that imply the risk of lowered quality, is a sign of reliability.

Think of a restaurant that doesn't accept reservations after it is all booked up, and where a table must be reserved for weeks in advance to eat there - of course, well. This immediately activates the principles of scarcity and social proof. This is an example of the power of saying no. Tip: in these places, there is always a spot for important people; those who could influence choosing other places. Rules are not universal and, like strategies, must be understood, embraced and interpreted before being executed.

There is also the "Yes trap". When we accept something that doesn't satisfy us, the principle of consistency takes over and we begin to make up false reasons to support the choice we have made. This emotional trick allows us to disregard the immediate stress of negotiation. We accept unsatisfactory conditions and the subsequent frustrations, because we try to rationalize the choice we've made.

Finally, we must align ourselves to the way in which our customers **measure success**. The Camel Theory ends the sale process with customer satisfaction, and this can only occur when the promise of a value transfer has been realized and all the interlocutors can affirm that it has been a success.

Measuring success is a task for top management or those who represent them. However, it's usually something more complex than just the personal goals of single individuals, which should be addressed anyway; it involves the whole organization. Thanks to the principle of authority, *top management* have defined the criteria that measure success, and will make sure that all those who participated in the project will adopt them as their own goals. Those who work on the customer must be able to understand and transmit them.

The "What" established a relationship between needs and benefits that was delivered by the functionalities of the proposition. The "Why" certified that these benefits were necessary for our customer and that they didn't have the option of not doing anything. The "Why Us" protected us from potential competitors, because we established that the functionalities that generate the benefit are part of our uniqueness. All this became concrete in the "When" phase, when the delivery times were established. In this phase we set the necessary goals for the "transfer of value", which is what happened after the sale, no matter whether we are talking putting a new plant into production, unpacking a product or the experience of a new service.

From a methodological standpoint, the "When" phase is associated with a presentation. In this case we don't mean a tool such as PowerPoint or Keynote. Rather we are describing a well-defined moment, when we will be able to meet the decision-makers and show them the work done, the information gathered, the commitments we will assume and the results we will deliver, in order to **obtain their approval**. Presentation skills, as well as other associated strategies, have been the object of many interesting studies. Some people, such as Nancy Duarte[46], have dedicated their entire career to studying how to make an effective presentation. Let's be inspired by this, but in summing up the generated value, let's also take into consideration the fact that a path has made and there is value is this. We must be able to speak about both the trip and the destinations: the mutual commitments. They both generate value. They are our story's end.

---

[46] Nancy Duarte, *Slide:ology*, O'Reilly Media US, 2008

THE CAMEL WAY[47]

Let's try to move from theory to practice. We have envisaged this chapter as a "Sales Cycle", a support tool that can accompany the seller step-by-step through all the elements of the Camel Theory, using the material available on www.thecameltheory.com.

The **Camel Way,** in its "design" variant, is the storyboard's creation with all the storytelling. It's a series of role-plays, where the participants (who are expert members of the company, in tune with the organization's values) create scenarios, which will be the multitude of stories that will be available to those who will be out in the field. The most effective version of any tale will be the one about successful cases, because they activate the principle of social proof[48]: people love to know that someone similar found themselves in a similar situation and succeeded. The

---

[47] CAMELWAY-MAP available on www.thecameltheory.com

[48] Robert Cialdini, *Influence. The Psychology of Persuasion,* 1984;

element of similarity is essential to make this work. The person we use as an example must have the same profile; it's even better if it's the same as the one we used for the creation of the proto-profile. However, let's not underestimate hypothetical situations: they help us to think about our profiles.

In its "execution" variant, the Camel Way is a metaphorical trip through the desert. To complete it, we must gradually fill in all the maps. You don't have to respect a strict order among the various way-points; however, we advise ticking each one off, before moving on to the next phase.

Prepare for the trip. Know the company and the people, and fill in the maps.

Know the people. Create a "PROFILE MAP" for each interlocutor. Identify their needs, even if they are not specific to the solution we want to propose, in this phase. To do this, we recommend taking the mentality of a beginner, so you avoid any assumptions, which may lead to misunderstandings. Advice: use social networks, and avoid trying to sell something straight after your first contact (this would trigger the *fight or fight* reaction). After making an appointment and introducing yourself and your company: **listen carefully and don't speak too much**. Excessive information, especially our listing your products or your company's qualities, may create confusion. Your interlocutor could become defensive, because they activated the association "Seller equals annoyance", and then they might give you information that they think will discourage you.

Data gathering. Note only the facts; i.e., the information that has been certified by our interlocutor (those that can trigger the principle of consistency) and that can be observed in his past actions and experiences. Don't overestimate assumptions. Ask many, many times, until you are certain about the main cause of the issue at hand. Our goal must be learning in order to put as much information as possible into our maps. Suggestion: always get permission to ask more questions or for another appointment, and always ask yourself who else you can speak to. The customers' POWER-MAP will hardly be composed of just one person.

WHAT-PHASE

- ✓ Identify the more suitable interlocutors to start the qualification. Create a PROFILE-MAP for each one to research the needs.

- ✓ Meet the customer, to verify the opportunity. We will have to identify a decision-maker or influencer, who we will use as our main reference. The maps for our reference must be much more detailed, so be sure to invest all of the necessary time. Rushing things at this point would compromise the entire sales cycle.

- ✓ Discuss the product/service generally and check if there is any blocking problem (technical, political or relational). Don't leave any potential deal-breaker pending. There is only one case where we may postpone a technical issue: when our competitive benefit come from the solution to that problem; in this case, we will keep it for the Why-Us phase.

- ✓ Build a relationship with our main reference. Obviously, it depends on the knowledge level between companies. If it's a new contact, the work will be long; however, without a relationship, it will be difficult to get information.
- ✓ Identify the needs. They are the results of the meeting(s). The needs that are discovered, through the relationship, complete the PROFILE-MAP and we can then start filling in the WHAT-MAP (the right-hand side). The left-hand side should have been filled during the design phase.
- ✓ Complete the maps. We have created the WHAT-MAP, from where we gleaned, at least, three points that express a relationship between the need and the benefit. This is the WHAT-LIST.

WHY-PHASE.

- ✓ Quantify. We quantified the (at least) three points of the WHAT-LIST, in terms of value for our interlocutor and his company.
- ✓ Obtain confirmation. Ask our interlocutor for confirmation of our assumptions, trying to obtain the "convincing" attribute.
- ✓ Look for a convincing event. We can apply the principle of authority, from which an event will

occur that will prompt the customer to do something to something.

- ✓ Find some sponsors. We have an influencer on our side, who is typically the one who will get the most benefit from our proposition. We know who is the decision-maker that we must persuade is and their profile is clear.

- ✓ Verify the timing. We acknowledged the times for the transfer of value. They are our product/service's standard times, including any customizations.

- ✓ Verify the investment. We have a commitment from our main reference that the benefit offers such value for the company that the investment is reasonably secure.

- ✓ Double check. We asked ourselves if the customer can "not do anything".

WHY-US-PHASE

- ✓ Check the decision-making process. We filled in the POWER-MAP and identified the decision-making process. We discovered which interlocutors favored us, who must be persuaded and who was against.

- ✓ Look for the competitors. Who are the potential competitors or other elements that could be obstacles? Let's make sure they don't have unique points that could offer benefits. If that is the case, let's prepare a strategy, based on perceived value or price.

- ✓ Verify uniqueness. We've connected our technological or model advantages with the relationship between need and benefit. Our interlocutors will confirm that.

- ✓ Perceive the value. Strengthen the effect of our uniqueness through storytelling, stressing customization. Make exclusivity stand out.

- ✓ Cement the organizations. Let's make sure that our interlocutors know "how" our company is the most suitable one to help them gain the advantages that we found in the various profiles.

WHEN-PHASE

- ✓ Share the timings. We certified the times for the transfer of value and we clearly expressed "how" our company is able to respect them, while leaving the benefit unchanged. Let's trigger a sense of urgency.

- ✓ Sum up the trip. We have the technical and managerial approval. Depending on the type of investment, this might occur after a presentation to the decision-makers. We can take care of that or our sponsor might do it. Make sure it includes the "story of the journey", and uses storytelling at the key points.

- ✓ Eliminate the risk of competitors. Theoretically, we have already done that in the previous phase, but no company with a purchasing process will enter a negotiation phase without two or three options. Typically, three companies are put on a *short-list*, and the top management will analyze them, along with the recommendations of the decision-maker and the buyers. Stress the qualification's results, to avoid unpleasant surprises.

- ✓ Measure success. We must find out why the top management chose us and what the success indicators will be. Satisfying them means building a relationship between the two organizations that will simplify future contracts. If we weren't the ones who made the presentation, or, if in that phase these elements weren't made clear, we must make sure that our reference finds out what they are and informs us.

Now we should have a signed order. Make sure you transmit the goals to the departments in charge of the "transfer of value" so that this can be a success for everyone. That means agreed times, the factors that determined the final choice and clear and measurable expectations. Give them a summary of the work done, including the factors that helped us to win. Make sure promises are kept. Asking for feedback helps to activate a virtuous cycle of common successes, based on a strong relationship; never underestimate the power of this step, even when the post-sales is simply entrusting a courier with a shipment. Think about how we feel, as consumers, when we order something and we receive all the information without asking. These things contribute to a trust relationship that is the basis of *brand awareness* and *user experience.*

Do not confuse experience with the simple passing of time. Look for the main cause of successes and failures; we can use this information to update our experience baggage and our storyboard. We can pass the information to those in charge of the design, so that they may be inspired. Let's improve constantly.

Conclusions

My original idea was to build a bridge between *business model* texts and *sales* ones. In the end, I would like this idea of the proposition to be a new point of view; an area where a message is generated about a value transfer, which is what we are paid for. What we think, our bright ideas that the business relies on, mean nothing if they are not accepted and "bought" by others.

The core of this method is qualification, which in my experience is element that is most neglected by those who work in the field. In all markets, the space dedicated to by banal products is already occupied. "Blue Ocean" and the "Purple Cow" strategies suggest specializing to create a market segment where our product/service can be a *leader.*

Our qualification adopts this philosophy – pushing a client to act. It identifies the functionalities that can satisfy their needs; but not all functionalities, only those who will make us stand out as unique. With a qualification process, our company, and we, will appear the most suitable for the (customer's) specific task. At this point, the customer organization will become our "blue ocean".

Qualification reduces the number of options, in order to simplify the decision-making process.

There's no difference between the design of a competitive advantage and the sale. Outside of research and development departments, if indeed they still exist, design and the realization of a proposition are continuously chasing each other. A successful organization makes sure that everyone puts into practice what was thought of: all resources move in the same direction. At the same time, however, the organization measures its results, in order to improve, which it does by changing and adapting.

Business deals are agreements between people; the personal component is crucial and we have tried to give scientific reasons for this statement. The particularities of the person who acts as our interlocutor are the central elements of this work, as well as the talent of those who must bring the proposition to the field. A talent serves the values and goals of the company it belongs to. All this is sales.

The relationship we build with our customers is the channel through which values are transmitted and *brand awareness* is created. The company's reputation is needed to make the promise influential. Investments made to create a competitive advantage (functionalities) must trigger others, those that the customer will make, to obtain a benefit. If the result is satisfying for both parties, a positive cycle will be started for all the actors.

In order for all this to happen, there must be a clear *leadership,* which defines the proposition. This *leadership* can only find fertile ground for its vision in a company that has all its elements balanced. That is a company that welcomes and includes the best talents and that is held together by shared values and ethics above all. It has a tendency towards change: endogenous for its constant improvement and exogenous to receive that which comes from the outside and which could be destructive.

Marco Lucchina

BIBLIOGRAPHY

Alexander Osterwalder - Yves Pigneur, *Business Model Canvas*, 2010.

Robert Cialdini, *Influence. The Psychology of Persuasion*, 1984

Marc Muchnick, *The Leadership Pill: The Missing Ingredient in Motivating People Today*, Free Press, 2003.

Gareth Morgan, *Images of Organization*, 1986

Leander Kahney, *Inside Steve's Brain*, 2008

Walter Isaacson, *Steve Jobs*, Simon & Schuster, 2011

Nancy Duarte & Patti Sanchez, *Illuminate*, Penguin Group UK, 2016

Nancy Duarte, *Slide:ology*, O'Reilly Media US, 2008

Osterwalder Pigneur Bernarda Smith, *Value Proposition Design*, 2014

W. Chan Kim - Renée Maunorgne, *Blue Ocean Strategy*, Harvard Business Review Press, 2005

Daniel Goleman, *Emotional Intelligence*, New York, NY;

England: Bantam Books, Inc., 1995

Philip Kotler, Kevin Keller, *Marketing Management*, 2007

Kenneth Blanchard, *The Leadership Pill: The Missing Ingredient in Motivating People Today*, Free Press, 2003.

Masaaki Imai, *Gemba Kaizen*, McGraw-Hill Education, 1997.

Tom & David Kelley, *Creative Confidence*, kindle edition.

Maud Besançon, *Le Haut Potentiel* Crèatif available on https://www.cairn.info/revue-enfance2-2010-1-page-77.htm

Martin Sykes, N.Malik, M. West, *Stories that Move Mountains: Storytelling & visual design*, Wiley, 2012

Seth Godin, *Purple Cow*, Portfolio, 2003

ABOUT THE AUTHOR

Marco Lucchina is a Chief Technology Officer, as well as a business and product strategist.

I have a degree in literature, but I have always worked with technology, since the moment I assembled my first computer on my own, until 2006, when my professional path led me to the discovery of «product management».

After a while, I also discovered the concept of emotional intelligence and for the ten years that followed, I studied, experimented and applied emotional stimuli to value propositions, people management and negotiations.

www.ingramcontent.com/pod-product-compliance
Lightning Source LLC
Chambersburg PA
CBHW031420210526
45464CB00005B/1981